Study Guide Part 1: Chapters 1-7

MW01045748

To Accompany

Accounting Principles
Fourth Canadian Edition

JERRY J. WEYGANDT Ph.D., C.P.A.

Arthur Andersen Alumni Professor of Accounting
University of Wisconsin – Madison
Madison, Wisconsin

DONALD E. KIESO Ph.D., C.P.A.

KPMG Peat Marwick Emeritus Professor of Accountancy
North Illinois University
DeKalb, Illinois

PAUL D. KIMMEL Ph.D., C.P.A.

University of Wisconsin – Milwaukee
North Illinois University
Milwaukee, Wisconsin

BARBARA TRENHOLM M.B.A., F.C.A.

University of New Brunswick
Fredericton, New Brunswick

VALERIE A. KINNEAR M.Sc. (Bus. Admin.), C.A.

Mount Royal College
Calgary, Alberta

Prepared by
CAROLE REID CLYNE C.M.A., M.Ed.

Centennial College
Toronto, Ontario

JOHN WILEY AND SONS CANADA, LTD

Copyright © 2007 by John Wiley & Sons Canada, Ltd

Copyright © 2005 by John Wiley & Sons Inc. All rights reserved. No part of this work covered by the copyrights herein may be reproduced or used in any form or by any means—graphic, electronic, or mechanical—without the prior written permission of the publisher.

Any request for photocopying, recording, taping or inclusion in information storage and retrieval systems of any part of this book shall be directed in writing to The Canadian Copyright Licensing Agency (Access Copyright). For an Access Copyright Licence, visit www.accesscopyright.ca or toll-free, 1-800-893-5777.

Care has been taken to trace ownership of copyright material contained in this text. The publishers will gladly receive any information that will enable them to rectify any erroneous reference or credit line in subsequent editions.

Library and Archives Canada Cataloguing in Publication

Reid Clyne, Carole
    Study guide to accompany Accounting principles, fourth Canadian edition, Jerry J. Weygandt ... [et al.] / Carole Reid Clyne.

Supplement to: Accounting principles.

ISBN 978-0-470-83947-8 (pt. 1).—ISBN 978-0-470-83948-5 (pt. 2)

1. Accounting—Problems, exercises, etc. I. Title.

HF5635.A3778 2006 Suppl. 1   657'.044   C2007-900433-4

Production Credits

Editorial Manager: Karen Staudinger
Publishing Services Director: Karen Bryan
Editorial Assistant: Sara Dam
Director of Marketing: Isabelle Moreau
Cover Design: Interrobang Graphic Design
Printing & Binding: Webcom Inc.

Printed and bound in Canada
10 9 8 7 6 5 4 3 2 1

John Wiley & Sons Canada Ltd.
6045 Freemont Blvd
Mississauga, ON
L5R 4J3
Visit our website at: www.wiley.ca

CONTENTS PART 1

TO THE STUDENT

This study guide will aid you significantly in your study of Accounting Principles, Fourth Canadian Edition, by Jerry J. Weygandt, Donald E. Kieso, Paul D. Kimmel, Barbara Trenholm and Valerie Kinnear. The material in the study guide is designed to reinforce your understanding of the principles and procedures presented in the textbook. It is important to recognize that the study guide is a supplement to and not a substitute for the textbook.

This study guide contains the following materials for each chapter in the textbook:

- Study objectives
- Preview of the chapter
- Chapter review of key points
- Demonstration problem and solution
- Multiple choice questions
- Matching exercise for key terms and definitions
- Exercises

Solutions to the review questions and exercises are provided at the end of each chapter to help you assess how well you understand the material. The solutions explain the reasoning behind the answer, so you get immediate feedback as to what, how, and why.

To benefit the most from this study guide, we recommend you take the following steps:

1. Carefully read the chapter material in the textbook.
2. Read the chapter preview and review in the study guide.
3. Take notes in class.
4. Answer the questions and exercises for the chapter in the study guide and compare your answers with the solutions provided. If you answer a question incorrectly, refer back to the textbook for a discussion of the point you missed.
5. Solve the end-of-chapter material in the textbook as assigned by your instructor.

The study guide should help you prepare for examinations. The chapter review points, class notes, and other materials will help you determine how well you can recall information presented in each chapter. When you have identified topics that you need to study further, return to the textbook for a complete discussion.

In addition to this study guide, the following supplementary materials are available from your bookstore or the publisher for use with the textbook Accounting Principles, Fourth Canadian Edition.

Special Student Supplements That Help You Get The Best Grade You Can

The Accounting Principles Resource Website

This site serves as a launching pad to numerous activities and resources for all students. You will find a series of study aids and practice tools: animated tutorials to help with key accounting concepts; interactive quizzes, an online glossary, and additional demonstration problems to help prepare for class and tests; and a comprehensive section on ethics in accounting. In addition, there are links to companies discussed in the text, downloadable resources such as a checklist of key figures and PowerPoint presentations, and much more.

www.wiley.com/canada/weygandt

WileyPLUS

Your instructor may be using *WileyPLUS*, an online suite of resources that includes a complete multi-media version of the text that will help you come to class better prepared for lectures, and allows you to track your progress throughout the course more easily. If so, you have access to a complete e-book with links to tools such as self-assessment quizzes and animated tutorials to help you study more efficiently. *WileyPLUS* is designed to provide instant feedback as you practise on your own. You can work through assignments with automatic grading or review custom-made class presentations featuring reading assignments, PowerPoint slides, and interactive simulations.

Working Papers

Working Papers are partially completed accounting forms for the end-of-chapter brief exercises, exercises, and problems. Journals, ledgers, T accounts, and other required working papers have been predetermined and included for each textbook assignment, so that you can redirect limited time to important accounting concepts rather than formatting.

City Cycle Practice Set

This practice set exposes you to a real-world simulation of maintaining a complete set of accounting records for a business. Business papers add a realistic dimension by enabling you to handle documents, cheques, invoices, and receipts that you would encounter in a small proprietorship. This practice set reinforces key concepts from Chapters 1 through 4 and allows you to apply the information you have learned. It is an excellent way to see how these concepts are all brought together to generate the accounting information that is essential in assessing the financial position and operating results of a company.

Suggestions for Effective Studying

Want to get better grades? Read on!

Good students have a system for studying. In the next few pages, we'll give you some guidelines that we think can help improve the way you study—not only in your accounting principles course, but in every course. If you need more specific help, we suggest you ask your instructor or consult a career counsellor at your school.

How to Use a Textbook

Textbooks often include material designed to help you study. It's worth your while to flip through a textbook and look for:

- **The Preface**. If an author has a point of view, you can find it here, along with notes on how the book is meant to be used.
- **The Table of Contents**. Reading the table of contents will help you understand how the topics covered in the book fit together.
- **Glossary**. The most important terms and ideas for you to know will be in the glossary, either at the end of each chapter or at the end of the book.
- **Appendices**. Found at the end of certain chapters, appendices contain such things as:
  - More difficult material.
  - Answers to selected problems.
  - Specimen financial statements.

How to Read a Chapter

Before Class: Skim

Unless you're told to know a chapter thoroughly by class time, it's a good idea just to skim it before class.

- Become familiar with the main ideas so that the lecture will make more sense to you.
- As you skim, ask yourself if you know something about the material.
- Keep any questions you have in mind for the lecture, so that you can listen for the answers.

In particular, look for:

- **Study Objectives**. These are what you will be expected to know—and be able to do or explain—by the end of the chapter.
- **Chapter-Opening Vignettes**. Each chapter opens with a brief story that reflects the topic of the chapter. The story or "vignette" will give you an idea of how accounting relates to your day-to-day life.
- **Boldface or *Italic* Terms**. These are important terms, concepts, or people.
- **Headings**. Read the major headings to see how the material fits together. How are the ideas related to each other? Do they make sense to you?
- **Summary**. A good summary repeats the main points and conclusions of the chapter, but it does not explain them. The summary usually matches up with the study objectives and introduction to the chapter.

After Class: Read

After skimming the chapter and attending class, you are ready to read the chapter in more detail.

- **Check for Meaning**. Ask yourself as you read if you understand what the material means.
- **Don't Skip the Tables, Figures, and Illustrations**. They contain important information that may be on a test. They may also offer a different perspective on the material and help to deepen your understanding of it.
- **Read the Sidebars and Feature Boxes**. These items are set off from the main text, either in the margin or in colour boxes. They may include real-world examples, amusing anecdotes, or additional material.
- **Review**. Read the chapter again, especially the parts you found difficult. Review the study objectives, chapter introduction, summary, and key terms to make sure you understand them.
- **End-of-Chapter Questions**. Do all the end-of-chapter questions, exercises, or problems. For the exercises and problems, make sure you have memorized which equations or rules apply and why. Do any practice problems assigned by your instructor, too. These problems will not only help you, but show you what kind of questions might be on a test. If you have trouble with any:
  - Review the part of the chapter that applies.
  - Look for similar questions and do them.
  - Ask yourself which concept or equation should be applied.
- **Use the Study Guide**. After you've read and studied the chapter, use the study guide to identify which areas you need to review in the text.

How to Take Notes

The ability to take notes is a skill, and one you can learn. First, a few practical tips:

- Arrive in class on time and don't leave early. You might miss important notes or assignments.
- Sit close enough to the instructor so you can hear him or her and read overhead transparencies.
- If you don't understand, ask questions.
- Do not read the text during class—you'll miss what the instructor is saying. Listen, take notes, and ask questions.

Now for the note-taking itself:

- **Listen for Ideas**. Don't try to write everything the instructor says. Instead, listen and take notes on the main ideas and any supporting ideas and examples. Make sure you include names, dates, and new terms. In accounting classes, take down all rules, equations, and theories, as well as every step in a demonstration problem.
- **Use Outlines**. Organize ideas into outlines. Indent supporting ideas under the main ones.
- **Abbreviate**. To help you write more quickly, use abbreviations, either standard ones or ones you make up. For example, leaving out vowels can sometimes help: Lvg out vwls can ...).
- **Leave Space**. Leave enough space in your notes so that you can add material if the instructor goes back to the topic or expands a problem later.

How to Use a Study Guide (In General)

A study guide is specific to the textbook you use. It can't replace the text; it can only point out places where you need more work. To use a study guide effectively:

- Use it only after you've read the chapter and reviewed your class notes.
- Ask yourself if you really understand the chapter's main points and how they relate to each other.
- Go back and reread the sections of your text that deal with any questions you missed. The text will not ask the same questions as the study guide, but it can help you to understand the material better. If that doesn't work, ask your instructor for help.
- Remember that a study guide can't cover any extra material that your instructor may lecture on in class.

How to Take Tests

Studying for a Test

Studying for tests is a process that starts with the first class and ends only with the last test. All through the semester, it helps to:

- Follow the advice we gave about reading a chapter and taking notes.
- Review your notes:
  - immediately after class. Clear up anything you can't read and circle important items while the lecture is still fresh in your mind.
  - periodically during the semester.
  - before a test.
- Use videotapes of lectures, if they have been made.

Now you're ready to do your final studying for a test. Leave as much time as you need, and study under the conditions that are right for you—alone or with a study group, in the library or another quiet place. It helps to schedule several short study sessions rather than to study all at one time.

- **Reread the chapter(s)**. Follow this system:
  - Most importantly, look for things you don't remember or don't understand.
  - Reinforce your understanding of the main ideas by rereading the introduction, study objectives, and summary.
  - Read the chapter from beginning to end.
- **Redo the problems**. Make sure you know which equation to apply or procedure to follow in different situations and why.
- **Test Yourself**. Cover up something you've just read and try to explain it to yourself—or to a friend—out loud.
- **Use Memory Tricks**. If you're having trouble remembering something—such as a formula or items in a list—try associating it with something you know or make a sentence out of the first letters.
- **Study with a Group**. Group study is helpful after you've done all your own studying. You can help each other with problems and by quizzing each other, but you'll probably just distract each other if you try to review a chapter together.

(**A Note about Cramming. Don't!** If you cram, you will probably only remember what you've read for a short time, and you'll have trouble knowing how to generalize from it. If you must cram, concentrate on the main ideas, the supporting ideas, main headings, boldface or italicized items, and study objectives.)

Taking a Test

After giving you some general tips, we'll focus on different types of tests: objective, problem, and essay.

- **Before the Test**

  - Make sure you eat well and get enough sleep.
  - If the instructor doesn't say in class what material will be covered or what kind of test it will be, ask.
  - Arrive early enough to get settled.
  - Bring everything you need—bluebook, pens, pencils, eraser, calculator—and the book, if it's an open-book test!

- **As You Begin the Test**

  - Read the instructions completely. Do you have to answer all of the questions? Do certain questions apply to others? Do some questions count more than others? Will incorrect answers be counted against you? \
  - Schedule your time. How many questions are there? Try to estimate how much time to leave for each section. If sections are timed so that you won't be able to return to them, make sure you leave enough time to decide which questions to answer.

- **Taking the Test**

  - Read each question completely as you come to it.
  - Answer the easier questions first and go back to the harder ones.
  - Concentrate on questions that count more.
  - Jot notes or equations in the margin if you think it will help.
  - Review your answers and don't change an answer unless you're sure it's wrong.

- **Dealing with Panic**

  - Relax. Do this by tightening and relaxing one muscle at a time.
  - Breathe deeply.
  - If you don't know an answer, go on to the next question.

Objective Tests
(Multiple choice, true-false, matching, completion or fill-in-the blanks)

- Watch out for words such as "always," "all," "every," "none," or "never." Very few things are always or never so. If a question or answer includes these words, be careful.

- If you are uncertain about a multiple choice answer, try to narrow the choices down to two and make an educated guess.

- On a matching test, match up the easy ones first. This will leave fewer possibilities for the hard ones.

- Make educated guesses for objective questions. If you really have no idea and a wrong answer will count against you, leave it blank.

Problem Tests

- If an equation is long, jot it down before you work on the problem.

- Remember that math builds one equation on another. If you can't remember a particular equation, try to remember how it was derived.

- Don't despair if you can't figure out what a question is calling for. Try to figure out part of it first. If that doesn't work, go on; sometimes a later question will jog your memory.

- If your instructor gives credit for partially correct problems, make sure you include the way you worked out a problem.

- Make sure that your calculator works before the test and, just in case, know how to do the problems without it. Sometimes you can hit the wrong button, so it helps to have a rough idea of what your calculator should be giving you.

Essay Tests

- Write a rough outline before you begin. If that takes too much time, just jot down all the things you want to say and then number them. Organize what you're going to say into groups of related ideas.

- Make a point in each paragraph. The easiest way is to make the point in the paragraph's first sentence and then back it up.

- Use examples, facts, and dates to back up what you are saying.

- Do what the question asks for. If it asks you to compare two things, for example, go back and forth between them; don't spend all your time on one of them.

- If you have no idea what to write, try to remember ideas that your instructor stressed in class and see if you can relate the question to those ideas.

- Check your time. If you're running out, write your last points down without explaining them; your teacher will at least know what you were going to explain.

c h a p t e r   1
Accounting in Action

study objectives >>

After studying this chapter, you should be able to:
1. Explain why accounting is important to accountants and non-accountants.
2. Explain generally accepted accounting principles and assumptions.
3. Use the accounting equation and explain the meaning of assets, liabilities, and owner's equity.
4. Analyze the effects of business transactions on the accounting equation.
5. Prepare financial statements.

Preview of Chapter 1

This chapter shows you that accounting is the system that produces useful financial information for decision making. The chapter is organized as follows:

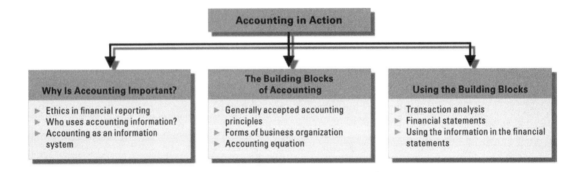

Why Is Accounting Important?

study objective 1

Explain why accounting is important to accountants and non-accountants.

Accounting is important because our economic system depends on highly transparent, reliable, and accurate financial reporting. Recently, corporate scandals have caused collapses of major companies, with a resulting loss of confidence in financial reporting.

These events have demanded that business behaviour in general, and accounting and auditing in particular, be guided by improved business practices, corporate governance, and accountability requirements.

Accounting, the language of business, must be understandable, useful, and truthful to be of any value. Whether you are self-employed or work for someone else in their business, learning how to read and interpret financial information is a valuable, relevant, and useful skill.

Ethics in Financial Reporting

Ethics are the standards of conduct by which a person's actions are judged right or wrong, honest or dishonest, fair or unfair. Effective financial reporting depends on sound ethical behaviour. Fortunately, most individuals in business are ethical.

Anyone involved in business decisions must consider the organization's interests when they make decisions. Accountants and other professionals have rules of conduct to guide their behaviour with each other and with the public. Many companies also have codes of conduct that outline their commitment to ethical behaviour in their internal and external relationships.

The following steps are used to outline ethical dilemmas:

1. Recognize an ethical situation and the ethical issues involved. (Use your personal and organization's code.)

2. Identify and analyze the main elements in the situation. (Identify persons or groups who may be harmed or benefited.)

3. Identify the alternatives and weigh the impact of each alternative on various stakeholders. (Select the most ethical alternative, considering all the consequences.)

Who Uses Accounting Information?

The information that the user of financial information needs depends on the kinds of decisions the user makes. These differences put the users into two broad groups: internal users and external users.

Internal Users

Internal users of accounting information plan, organize, and run businesses. They include marketing managers, production supervisors, finance directors, and company officers. All these internal users answer important questions about running the business. These questions must be asked and answered on a timely basis to provide information when needed.

External Users

External users work for other organizations but have interests in the financial position and performance of a company. They include investors, creditors, taxing authorities, regulatory agencies, labour unions, customers, and economic planners outside the business.

Accounting as an Information System

Accounting is an information system that identifies, records, and communicates the economic events of an organization to interested users.

1. **Identification** involves selecting events that are considered evidence of economic activity relevant to a particular organization. For example, the sale of sporting goods, the sale of telephone services to a customer, or the payment of wages to an employee is considered an economic event.

2. **Recording** involves keeping a systematic, chronological diary of events measured in dollars and cents. Classifying and summarizing economic events is also part of recording. Recording total sales of sporting equipment in a particular store location is an example of classifying or summarizing.

3. **Communication** of information results from identifying and recording economic activities. Accounting reports, the most common of which are financial statements, are prepared and distributed to interested users. Communication of financial information is recorded in a standardized way. Similar transactions are accumulated and totalled. This grouping together is said to be reported in aggregate.

An important part of communicating economic events is the accountant's ability and responsibility to analyze and interpret the reported information. By presenting recorded data in aggregate, the accounting information system simplifies a large number of transactions. As a result, the company's activities are easier to understand and more meaningful.

The Building Blocks of Accounting

The accounting profession has developed a body of theory based on principles and assumptions. Accountants follow certain standards to report financial information.

Generally Accepted Accounting Principles

Generally accepted accounting principles (GAAP) are a common set of standards that are generally accepted and universally practised. They have developed over time in response to tradition, experience, and user needs. They recommend how to report economic events.

study objective 2

Explain generally accepted accounting principles and assumptions.

The Canadian Institute of Chartered Accountants (CICA), through an Accounting Standards Board (AcSB), has the main responsibility for the development of GAAP in Canada. GAAP, published in the CICA Handbook, are not static. They change over time so that they continue to provide information relevant to decision-making as the business environment changes.

AcSB has created GAAP after a long process of consultation with organizations and individuals who are interested or affected by the principles. Its work is supervised by an independent Accounting Standards Oversight Council (AcSOC).

Internationally, accounting standards differ from country to country. The International Accounting Standards Board (IASB) has been trying to reduce the differences in accounting practices by encouraging the use of one set of international standards. Canadian standard setters have recently decided that publicly traded companies must adopt international financial reporting standards (IFRS) by 2010.

Cost Principle
We need to have a good understanding of generally accepted accounting principles to prepare and understand accounting information. One of the most basic principles is the **cost principle**. It states that assets should be recorded at their original historic cost. Cost is the value exchanged at the time something is acquired, and it is definite and verifiable.

Assumptions
When generally accepted accounting principles are developed, certain assumptions that create a foundation for the accounting process are made.

- **Going concern assumption**: Going concern assumes that the organization will continue to operate in the foreseeable future. It also presumes that a company will operate year after year.

- **Monetary unit assumption**: This assumption requires that only transaction data that can be expressed in terms of money be included in the accounting records. The monetary unit assumption also assumes that the unit of measure (for example, Canadian dollar, British pound) remains sufficiently constant over time.

- **Economic entity assumption**: This assumption requires that the activities of the entity be kept separate and distinct from the activities of its owner and all other economic entities.

Forms of Business Organization

A business may be organized as a proprietorship, partnership, or corporation.

- A **proprietorship** is a business owned by one person. There is no legal distinction between the business as an economic unit and the owner.

- A **partnership** is a business owned by two or more persons associated as partners. Partnership activities must be kept separate from the personal activities of each partner.

- A **corporation** is a business organized as a separate legal entity under provincial or federal corporation law. Its ownership is divided into transferable shares. Corporations that are listed on the Canadian stock exchange are public corporations. Private corporations do not issue shares to the public; their shares are privately owned.

- **Income trusts** are special or limited purpose corporations that are set up specifically to invest in income-producing assets.

Accounting Equation

The accounting equation is:

study objective 3

Use the accounting equation and explain the meaning of assets, liabilities, and owner's equity.

Assets = Liabilities + Owner's Equity

The accounting equation is the same for all economic entities regardless of size, nature of business, or form of business organization. This equation is the basis for recording and summarizing the economic events of a company. The categories in the accounting equation are as follows:

- **Assets** are resources owned by a business (what a business owns). Every asset is capable of providing future services or benefits since assets are used in the activities of the business.

- **Liabilities** are creditors' claims against assets (what a business owes). They are the existing debts and obligations of the business.

- **Owner's Equity** is the ownership claim of owner(s) on total assets. Owner's equity is also referred to as residual equity since it is equal to assets minus liabilities. The main purpose of a business is to generate income from business activities and so increase equity. The components of equity are as follows:
  - Investments are the assets the owner puts into the business. Investments **increase** owner's equity and also increase assets.
  - Drawings are withdrawals of cash or other assets by the owner for personal use. Drawings **decrease** owner's equity and also decrease assets.
  - **Net Income or net loss is determined by revenues and expenses:**
        When revenues are greater than expenses = Net Income
        When expenses are greater than revenues = Net Loss
  - Revenues result from the sale of goods or services by a business. Revenues **increase** owner's equity.
  - Expenses are the costs of assets consumed and services used in earning revenue. Expenses **decrease** owner's equity.

  The ending balance in the owner's equity account, after adding investments and revenues and deducting drawings and expenses, is referred to as **Owner's Capital**.

Accounting Equation Distinctions by Type of Business Organization

The main distinction between the forms of business organizations are found in the terminology used to name the equity section and the account, and in the reporting of the owner's investments and withdrawals.

In a proprietorship, the equity is termed owner's equity. In a partnership, the equity is termed partners' equity because there may be two or more owners. In a corporation, the owners are called shareholders and the equity is called shareholders' equity. In an income trust, the owners are the unitholders and the equity is called unitholders' equity.

In both proprietorships and partnerships, equity is reported for each respective owner in a one-line capital account. For a corporation, the investments by the shareholders are called share capital. Retained earnings are the accumulated earnings of the corporation that have not been paid out to shareholders. Dividends are withdrawals of assets by the shareholders.

Income trusts, a special form of corporation, has a different equity section. It distributes any equity that it does not need for operations to its unitholders. Since most of its earnings are distributed, it does not use a retained earnings account. Instead, it uses the term undistributed income since that income will eventually be distributed to unitholders.

Using the Building Blocks

study objective 4

Analyze the effects of business transactions on the accounting equation.

Transactions are the economic events of a business. They may be identified as either external or internal transactions.

Each transaction must be analyzed in terms of its effect on the components of the accounting equation, including the specific items affected and the amount of the change in each item. The change in each item must be recorded in the accounting process. If a transaction has no effect on the accounting equation, it is not recorded in the accounting process; however, it could still be a business transaction (for example, answering a customer query).

Each transaction has a dual effect on the equation. Therefore, both sides of the equation must always be equal. For example, if an individual asset is increased, there must be a corresponding
1. decrease in another asset, or
2. increase in a liability, or
3. increase in owner's equity.

A table may be prepared to show the cumulative effect of transactions on the accounting equation. The summary demonstrates that
1. each transaction must be analyzed in terms of its effect on the three components of the equation, and
2. the two sides of the equation must always be equal.

Illustration 1-7 in the text demonstrates the effects of 10 transactions on Softbyte's accounting equation. Observe how total assets ($18,050) equal total liabilities plus owner's equity ($1,600 + $16,450 = $18,050).

Regardless of the nature of the transaction, it is a fundamental rule of accounting that the accounting equation must always balance. That is, total assets must always equal total liabilities plus owner's equity.

Financial Statements

study objective 5

Prepare financial statements.

Four financial statements are prepared from the summarized accounting data:

1. An **income statement** presents the revenues and expenses and resulting net income (or net loss) of a business for a specific period of time.

2. A **statement of owner's equity** summarizes the changes in owner's equity for a specific period of time.

3. A **balance sheet** reports the assets, liabilities, and owner's equity of a business at a specific date.

4. A **cash flow statement** summarizes information concerning the cash inflows (receipts) and outflows (payments) for a specified period of time.

The financial statements are interrelated because:
*   Net income shown on the income statement is added to the owner's capital in the statement of owner's equity. Net loss is subtracted from the owner's capital.
*   Owner's capital at the end of the reporting period shown in the statement of owner's equity is reported in the balance sheet.
*   The amount of cash shown on the balance sheet is reported in the cash flow statement.

In the income statement, revenues are listed first, followed by expenses. If a business has more than one source of revenue, the revenue items are listed separately and then totalled. Similarly, expenses are listed separately and totalled. Total expense is subtracted from total revenue to calculate net income (or net loss).

The statement of owner's equity shows the owner's capital at the beginning of the period, additional investments of assets by the owner, net income (or net loss) for the period, owner's drawings, and the resulting amount of owner's capital at the end of the period.

In the balance sheet, assets are listed first, followed by liabilities and owner's equity. Like the income statement, the balance sheet shows totals for each component of the accounting equation: total assets, total liabilities, and owner's capital. Note that owner's capital as reported in the balance sheet must agree with the amount calculated as the ending balance on the statement of owner's equity.

The cash flow statement reports the sources, uses, and net increase or decrease in cash. Chapter 17 will examine in detail how this statement is prepared.

Using the Information in the Financial Statements

Public corporations issue their financial statements and supplementary materials in the form of annual reports. These reports are documents that include useful financial and non-financial information about the company. The statements of public companies are audited and also include the auditor's report. There is also a statement of management responsibility for the statements.

Private corporations do not issue their statements to the public; however, their statements must be prepared according to generally accepted accounting principles.

Demonstration Problem (SO 5)

Prepare a balance sheet for the Morse Soybean Company on December 31, 2008, using the following list of accounts.

Accounts Payable	$4,000
Accounts Receivable	3,500
Automobile	4,500
Cash	6,000
Equipment	7,000
J. Morse, Capital	?
Notes Payable	6,500
Salaries Payable	2,000
Supplies	2,500

Solution to Demonstration Problem

MORSE SOYBEAN COMPANY
Balance Sheet
December 31, 2008

Assets

Cash	$ 6,000
Accounts Receivable	3,500
Supplies	2,500
Equipment	7,000
Automobile	4,500
Total assets	$23,500

Liabilities and Owner's Equity

Liabilities	
Accounts Payable	$ 4,000
Salaries Payable	2,000
Notes Payable	6,500
Total liabilities	12,500
Owner's Equity	
J. Morse, Capital	11,000
Total liabilities and owner's equity	$23,500

Review Questions and Exercises

Multiple Choice

Circle the letter that best answers each of the following statements.

1. (SO 1) Which of the following is not part of the accounting process?

   a. Recording
   b. Identifying
   c. Financial decision-making
   d. Communicating

2. (SO 1) Internal users of accounting data include:

   a. economic planners.
   b. investors.
   c. customers.
   d. company officers.

3. (SO 1) Questions asked by external users may include:

   a. What is the cost of manufacturing each unit?
   b. Is the company earning satisfactory income?
   c. Which product line is more profitable?
   d. Is there sufficient cash to pay the bills?

4. (SO 1) An external user of information, like a labour union, may want to know:

    a whether the company is operating according to provincial regulations.

    b. whether the company will honour its product warranties.

    c. whether the company can pay increased wages and benefits.

    d. whether the company respects the tax laws.

5. (SO 1) Ethics are standards of conduct by which one's actions are judged as:

    a. right or wrong.

    b. honest or dishonest.

    c. fair or unfair.

    d. all of the above.

6. (SO 1) When ethical behaviour is practised in accounting, users are assured that accounting information is:

    a. credible and reliable.

    b. significant and organized.

    c. ineffective and inconsistent.

    d. similar to the user's ethics.

7. (SO 2) The organization(s) primarily responsible for establishing generally accepted accounting principles is (are) the:

	Canadian Institute of Chartered Accountants	Provincial securities commissions
a.	no	no
b.	yes	no
c.	no	yes
d.	yes	yes

8. (SO 2) The monetary unit assumption:

    a. provides that the unit of measure fluctuates over time.

    b. is unimportant in applying the cost principle.

    c. is only used for financial statements of banks.

    d. requires that only transaction data that can be expressed in terms of money be included in the accounting records of the economic entity.

9. (SO 2) A proprietorship is a business:

    a. owned by one person.

    b. owned by two or more persons.

    c. organized as a separate legal entity under provincial corporation law.

    d. owned by a government agency.

10. (SO 2) The unitholders of the income trust:

    a. must pay income taxes on the cash paid to them.

    b. do not pay taxes on income received.

    c. do not receive income since income is for operating expenses.

    d. receive a distribution of equity before operating expenses are paid.

11. (SO 3) The equity section of the income trust will show the following account:

    a. Retained Earnings.
    b. Shareholders' Equity.
    c. Undistributed Income.
    d. Capital Account.

12. (SO 3) A net loss will result during a time period when:

    a. assets exceed liabilities.
    b. assets exceed owner's equity.
    c. expenses exceed revenues.
    d. revenues exceed expenses.

13. (SO 3) All of the following accounts normally have credit balances except:

    a. revenue accounts.
    b. asset accounts.
    c. liability accounts.
    d. owner's capital account.

14. (SO 4) If a liability has increased, most likely you have:

    a. paid cash for an expense.
    b. exchanged an item for a new one.
    c. incurred an expense to be paid at a later date.
    d. invested cash in the business.

15. (SO 4) A company might carry on many activities that do not represent business transactions such as:

    a. borrowing money from a bank.
    b. placing an order for merchandise with a supplier.
    c. using office supplies.
    d. paying wages.

16. (SO 4) An example of an internal transaction is the:

    a. payment of monthly rent.
    b. hiring of employees.
    c. sale of pizza puffs to customers.
    d. use of paper, pens, and other office supplies.

17. (SO 4) The Caruzo Uptown Grill receives a bill of $400 from the Erml Advertising Agency. The owner, John Caruzo, is postponing payment of the bill until a later date. The effect on specific items in the accounting equation is:

    a. a decrease in Cash and an increase in Accounts Payable.
    b. a decrease in Cash and an increase in Revenue Earned.
    c. an increase in Accounts Payable and an increase in Advertising Expense.
    d. a decrease in Accounts Payable and an increase in Revenue Earned.

18. (SO 4) The Nagy Company is owned by Lynn Nagy. Jim James, the inventory clerk, indicates that $975 of supplies were used during the period. The effect on specific items in the accounting equation is:

    a. a decrease in Supplies and an increase in Supplies Expense.
    b. a decrease in Cash and an increase in Supplies.
    c. an increase in Accounts Payable and a decrease in Supplies.
    d. an increase in Supplies Payable and a decrease in Revenue Earned.

19. (SO 4) Doug Foerch, owner of the Poindexter Company, withdraws $500 in cash for personal use. The effect on specific items in the accounting equation is:

    a. an increase in Accounts Receivable and an increase in D. Foerch, Drawings.
    b. an increase in Salary Expense and a decrease in Cash.
    c. an increase in D. Foerch, Capital and a decrease in Cash.
    d. an increase in D. Foerch, Drawings and a decrease in Cash.

20. (SO 4) Jeanie Company purchases $600 of equipment from Mundelein Company for cash. The effect on the components of the accounting equation of Jeanie Company is:

    a. an increase in assets and liabilities.
    b. a decrease in assets and liabilities.
    c. no change in total assets.
    d. an increase in assets and a decrease in liabilities.

21. (SO 4) The Vessely Company has the following at September 17: assets $13,000; liabilities $8,000; and owner's equity $5,000. On September 18, Vessely Company receives $500 of cash revenue and earns $200 of revenue on credit. Mike McEllen, the only worker that day, works 8 hours and receives a wage rate of $10 per hour. Mike will not get paid until September 21. No other transactions occur during the day. At the end of September 18 the new totals are:

	Assets	Liabilities	Equity
a.	$13,500	$7,880	$5,620
b.	$12,500	$8,000	$4,500
c.	$13,500	$8,120	$5,380
d.	$13,700	$8,080	$5,620

22. (SO 5) As of December 31, 2008, Morley Company has liabilities of $5,000 and owner's equity of $7,000. Morley Company earned revenues of $23,000 during the year ended December 31, 2008. What are the assets for Morley Company as of December 31, 2008?

    a. $2,000
    b. $12,000
    c. $25,000
    d. $35,000

23. (SO 5) The statement that reports revenues and expenses is the:

    a. income statement.
    b. balance sheet.
    c. statement of owner's equity.
    d. cash flow statement.

24. (SO 5) Morreale Beaver Company buys a $12,000 van on credit. The transaction will affect the:

    a. income statement only.
    b. balance sheet only.
    c. income statement and statement of owner's equity.
    d. income statement, statement of owner's equity, and balance sheet.

25. (SO 5) The financial statement that summarizes the financial position of a company is the:

    a. income statement.
    b. balance sheet.
    c. operating statement.
    d. statement of owner's equity.

26. (SO 5) Which of the following would not appear on the Latourneau Company's balance sheet?

    a. Accounts Receivable
    b. M. Latourneau, Capital
    c. Utilities Expense
    d. Wages Payable

27. (SO 5) On a balance sheet, accounts would be classified in the following order:

    a. assets, owner's equity, liabilities.
    b. liabilities, owner's equity, assets.
    c. assets, liabilities, owner's equity.
    d. owner's equity, assets, liabilities.

Matching

Match each term with its definition by writing the appropriate letter in the space provided.

Terms

____ 1. Revenues

____ 2. Statement of owner's equity

____ 3. Owner's equity

____ 4. Balance sheet

____ 5. Monetary unit assumption

____ 6. Income statement

Definitions

a. Economic events of the company recorded by accountants.

b. The process of identifying, recording, and communicating the economic information of an organization to interested users.

c. The gross increases in owner's equity resulting from business activities entered into for the purpose of earning income.

d. Resources owned by the business.

e. Reports the assets, liabilities, and owner's equity of a business at a specific date.

_____ 7. Economic entity assumption

_____ 8. Assets

_____ 9. Accounting

_____ 10. Transactions

_____ 11. Expenses

_____ 12. Liabilities

_____ 13. Generally accepted
         accounting principles

_____ 14. Cost principle

_____ 15. Going concern assumption

f. The premise that the organization will continue to operate in the foreseeable future.

g. Presents the revenues and expenses and resulting net income of a company for a specific period of time.

h. Cost of assets consumed or services used in the process of earning revenue.

i. Creditors' claims on total assets.

j. Ownership claim on total assets.

k. Summarizes the changes in owner's equity for a specific period of time.

l. Requires that only transaction data that can be expressed in terms of money be included in the accounting records of the economic entity.

m. States that economic events can be identified with a particular unit of accountability.

n. States that assets should be recorded at their historical cost.

o. An accepted set of standards used by accountants in reporting economic events.

Exercises

E1-1   (SO 3) Some amounts are omitted in each of the following financial statements.

INCOME STATEMENT
Year Ended December 31, 2008

	Tang Company	June Company	Diana Company
Revenues	$48,000	$ (d)	$82,000
Expenses	(a)	52,000	64,000

STATEMENT OF OWNER'S EQUITY
Year Ended December 31, 2008

	Tang Company	June Company	Diana Company
Capital, January 1	$ (b)	$45,000	$50,000
Net income	15,000	24,000	(g)
Drawings	12,000	(e)	17,000
Capital, December 31	33,000	54,000	(h)

BALANCE SHEET
December 31, 2008

	Tang Company	June Company	Diana Company
Total assets	$75,000	$ (f)	$91,000
Total liabilities	(c)	56,000	40,000
Total owner's equity	33,000	54,000	(i)

Instructions
Determine the missing amounts and indicate your answers in the spaces provided below.

(a) ———————————   (d) ———————————   (g) ———————————

(b) ———————————   (e) ———————————   (h) ———————————

(c) ———————————   (f) ———————————   (i) ———————————

E1-2   (SO 4) On March 1, Laurie Fiala opened the Wahoo Beauty Salon. During the first month, the following selected transactions occurred:
1.   Deposited $5,000 cash in the City Bank in the name of the business.
2.   Paid $800 cash for beauty supplies.
3.   Purchased equipment at a cost of $12,000, paying $2,000 in cash and the balance on account.
4.   Received $1,200 cash for services performed.
5.   Paid $500 cash as a salary to a beautician.
6.   Withdrew $400 cash for personal expenses.

Instructions

Prepare a tabular summary of the transactions, using the following column headings: Cash; Supplies; Equipment; Accounts Payable; L. Fiala, Capital; L. Fiala, Drawings; Revenue; and Expenses. Calculate the total of the columns after all transactions have been recorded.

Trans-action		Assets			= Liabilities +		Owner's Equity			
	Cash +	Supplies +	Equipment	=	Accounts Payable	Fiala, + Capital	Fiala, – Drawings	+ Revenue	– Expenses	
1										
2										
3										
4										
5										
6										

E1-3   (SO 5) Selected financial statement items for the Geimer Company are presented below:

a.   Accounts Payable
b.   Service Revenue
c.   B. Geimer, Capital, Jan. 1, 2008
d.   Rent Expense
e.   Supplies
f.   Advertising Expense
g.   B. Geimer, Capital, Dec. 31, 2008
h.   Land
i.   Utilities Expense
j.   B. Geimer, Drawings
k.   Net Income
l.   Salaries Payable

Instructions

Indicate the financial statement(s) in which each item should be reported using the following code number(s): (1) Income statement for the year ended December 31, 2008, (2) Statement of owner's equity for the year ended December 31, 2008, and (3) Balance sheet, December 31, 2008. (Note: More than one code number may be required for an item.)

Item	Financial Statement	Item	Financial Statement	Item	Financial Statement
a.		e.		i.	
b.		f.		j.	
c.		g.		k.	
d.		h.		l.	

E1-4   (SO 5) On December 1, Cui Tu left for China on a business trip. She gave her independent accountant, Melissa Vialva, owner of the Vialva Accounting Company, $2,000 for work that was to be completed in that month. Ms. Vialva spent $600 of the money received on expenses, which she paid in cash in the month of December. The work was completed in December.

Instructions
From the point of view of the Vialva Accounting Company, state the following:

(a) The total effect that the receipt of the $2,000 would have on the balance sheet equation.

_____

(b) The effect the payment of $600 would have on the balance sheet equation.

_____

(c) The amount by which income would be increased for the month if that was the only job that the Vialva Accounting Company completed in December.

_____

E1-5   (SO 5) The Zaboca Company has the following results:

	2007	**Increase/Decrease**	**2008**
Revenue	$10,000	(a)	$20,000
Expenses	(b)	$15,000 increase	(c)
Net Income (Loss)	$5,000	(d)	(e)

	Beginning 2007	**Increase/Decrease**	**Ending 2007**
Assets	$700,000	(f)	(g)
Liabilities	$500,000	$150,000 increase	(h)
Owner's Equity	(i)	(j)	(k)

	Beginning 2008	**Increase/Decrease**	**Ending 2008**
Assets	(l)	(m)	(n)
Liabilities	(o)	$200,000 decrease	(p)
Owner's Equity	(q)	(r)	(s)

Assuming the owner invested $50,000 in the business in 2007 and withdrew $75,000 in 2008, enter the missing amounts in the spaces below.

(a)	(h)	(o)
(b)	(i)	(p)
(c)	(j)	(q)
(d)	(k)	(r)
(e)	(l)	(s)
(f)	(m)	
(g)	(n)	

E1-6   (SO 3) You are preparing for a group discussion on different types of business organizations. Your group has to do an in-class presentation (three minutes or less) that explains the differences in the flow of net income to the owners of the types of business organizations below:

> Proprietorship
> Partnership
> Corporation
> Income trust

Instructions
Prepare point-form notes for your presentation.

_____

_____

_____

_____

_____

_____

_____

_____

_____

Solutions to Review Questions and Exercises

Multiple Choice

1. (c)   Accounting is defined as the process of identifying, recording, and communicating economic events of an organization to interested users. The interested users then make financial decisions based on the information provided.

2. (d)   Economic planners, customers, and investors are external users of accounting data. Company officers, managers, and employees are internal users of accounting data.

3. (b)   External users would want to find out if the company is earning satisfactory income. Internal users would need to know costs of manufacturing, profitability of product lines, and the cash required to pay the company's bills.

4. (c)   Labour unions are external users of accounting information. They wish to know whether the owners can pay increased wages and benefits—important items in the union contract.

5. (d)   Ethics are standards that cover all of the choices listed.

6. (a)   When ethical standards are put into practice, users of accounting information are assured of credible and reliable data.

7. (b)   The Canadian Institute of Chartered Accountants is the organization primarily responsible for establishing generally accepted accounting principles.

8. (d)   The monetary unit assumption requires that only transaction data that can be expressed in terms of money be included in the accounting records of the economic entity. Choice (a) is false because it assumes that the unit of measure remains sufficiently constant over time. Choice (b) is incorrect because the monetary unit assumption is vital in applying the cost principle. Choice (c) is incorrect because this assumption is used for all types of entities.

9. (a)   A proprietorship is a business owned by only one person.

10. (a)   Unitholders pay income taxes on the cash they receive from the earnings of the income trust.

11. (c)   The term undistributed income is used instead of "retained earnings" for earnings that the trust intends to distribute.

12. (c)   A net loss will result when expenses exceed revenues. Net income results when revenues exceed expenses.

13. (b)   Asset accounts normally have debit balances.

14. (c)   An expense to be paid at a later date would increase a liability (accounts payable).

15. (b)   Borrowing from a bank, using office supplies, and paying wages are all recognized as business transactions, thus (a), (c), and (d) are incorrect. Placing an order for merchandise with a supplier is not recognized as a business transaction even though it may lead to a business transaction when the merchandise is delivered by the supplier.

16. (d)   The use of office supplies is an internal transaction because an outside party is not involved when the office supplies are used. Answers (a) and (c) involve outside parties and are, therefore, external transactions. Choice (b) is not a transaction.

17. (c)   The transaction is an advertising expense that has been incurred on account. Thus, the transaction increases Advertising Expense and increases the liability Accounts Payable.

18. (a)   The using up of supplies is an expense. Thus, the transaction decreases the asset Supplies and increases the Supplies Expense account.

19. (d) The withdrawal of cash by an owner for personal use reduces cash and increases the owner's drawings account. Drawings do not result in either an expense or a receivable.

20. (c) The transaction results in an increase in the asset Equipment and an equal decrease in the asset Cash. Therefore, there is no change in total assets.

21. (d) The effects of the transactions are summarized below.

	Assets	=	Liabilities	+	Owner's Equity
September 17	$13,000		$8,000		$5,000
Cash revenue	+ 500				+ 500
Credit revenue	+ 200				+ 200
Wage expense			+ 80		− 80
September 18	$13,700	=	$8,080	+	$5,620

22. (b) The balance sheet equation states Assets = Liabilities + Owner's Equity. Thus, if liabilities are $5,000 and owner's equity is $7,000, assets must equal $12,000. The revenue is already in the December 31, 2008, totals and therefore is not relevant to the answer.

23. (a) The income statement reports revenues and expenses as well as net income. The balance sheet reports assets, liabilities, and owner's equity. The statement of owner's equity explains the changes in owner's equity. The cash flow statement shows cash flows.

24. (b) The transaction represents an increase in assets of $12,000 and an increase in liabilities of an equal amount. The transaction causes a change in balance sheet items only.

25. (b) The balance sheet reports the financial position of a company. The income statement presents revenues and expenses. The statement of owner's equity explains the changes in owner's equity that have occurred during a given period of time.

26. (c) Accounts receivable, M. Latourneau, Capital, and Wages payable are all balance sheet items. Thus, (a), (b), and (d) are incorrect. Utilities expense is an item that is reported on the income statement.

27. (c) Assets, liabilities, owner's equity.

Matching

1.	c.	6.	g.	11.	h.
2.	k.	7.	m.	12.	i.
3.	j.	8.	d.	13.	o.
4.	e.	9.	b.	14.	n.
5.	l.	10.	a.	15.	f.

Exercises

E1-1

(a)	$33,000	(Revenues $48,000 – Net income $15,000)
(b)	$30,000	(Capital, Dec.31 $33,000 + Drawings $12,000 – Net income $15,000)
(c)	$42,000	(Assets $75,000 – Owner's equity $33,000)
(d)	$76,000	(Expenses $52,000 + Net income $24,000)
(e)	$15,000	(Capital, Jan.1 $45,000 + Net income $24,000 – Capital, Dec.31 $54,000)
(f)	$110,000	(Liabilities $56,000 + Owner's equity $54,000)
(g)	$18,000	(Revenues $82,000 – Expenses $64,000)
(h)	$51,000	(Capital, Jan.1 $50,000 + Net income $18,000 - Drawings $17,000)
(i)	$51,000	(Assets $91,000 – Liabilities $40,000)

E1-2

Trans-action	Assets			= Liabilities +		Owner's Equity			
				Accounts	Fiala,	Fiala,			
	Cash +	Supplies +	Equipment =	Payable	+ Capital	– Drawings	+ Revenue	– Expenses
1	+$5,000				+ $5,000			
2	– 800	+ $ 800						
3	– 2,000		+$12,000	+$10,000				
4	+1,200						+ $1,200	
5	– 500							– $500
6	– 400					– $400		
	$2,500	+ $ 800	+ $12,000	$10,000	+ $5,000	– $400	+ $1,200	– $500

E1-3

Item	Financial Statement	Item	Financial Statement	Item	Financial Statement
a.	3	e.	3	i.	1
b.	1	f.	1	j.	2
c.	2	g.	2, 3	k.	1, 2
d.	1	h.	3	l.	3

E1-4

(a) Increase in Cash $2,000. Increase in Revenue $2,000.
(b) Decrease in Cash $600. Increase in Expense $600.
(c) Net Income for December $1,400.

E1-5

(a)	$10,000 increase	(h)	$650,000	(o)	$650,000
(b)	$5,000	(i)	$200,000	(p)	$450,000
(c)	$20,000	(j)	$55,000 increase	(q)	$255,000
(d)	$5,000 decrease	(k)	$255,000	(r)	$75,000 decrease
(e)	$0	(l)	$905,000	(s)	$180,000
(f)	$205,000 increase	(m)	$275,000 decrease		
(g)	$905,000	(n)	$630,000		

E1-6

- Net income is the amount by which revenue is greater than expenses.
- The net income of a proprietor is totally owned by one person.
- The net income of a partnership is owned by the partners (two or more persons) with each person sharing in the proportion of his or her investment.
- The net income of a corporation may be retained by the company as Retained Earnings or distributed to shareholders as Dividends.
- The net income of an income trust may be retained by the trust as Undistributed Income or distributed to the unitholders as long as it is not needed for operational expenses.

chapter 2
The Recording Process

study objectives >>

After studying this chapter, you should be able to:
1. Define debits and credits and illustrate how they are used to record business transactions.
2. Describe the basic steps in the recording process, explain what a journal is, and journalize business transactions.
3. Explain what a ledger is and post journal entries.
4. Explain the purpose of a trial balance and prepare one.

Preview of Chapter 2

In Chapter 1 we used the accounting equation to analyze business transactions. The combined effects of these transactions were presented in a tabular form. This chapter introduces and illustrates the basic procedures that are used to journalize, post, and summarize transaction data. This chapter is organized as follows:

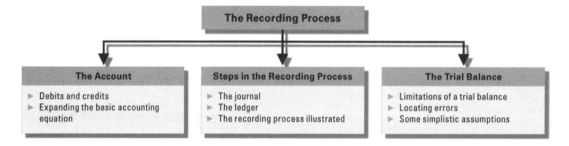

The Account

An **account** is an individual accounting record of increases and decreases in a specific asset, liability, or owner's equity item.

In its simplest form, an account consists of (1) the title of the account, (2) a left or debit side, and (3) a right or credit side. Together, these parts resembles the letter T, therefore the account form is called a **T account**. The T account will be used to explain basic accounting relationships.

Debits and Credits

study objective 1

Define debits and credits and illustrate how they are used to record business transactions.

The term **debit** indicates left, and the term **credit** indicates right. Entering an amount on the left side of a T account is called debiting the account. An entry on the right side of a T account is called crediting the account.

Debits to the left and credits to the right is an accounting custom or rule. This rule is used for all accounts. When the totals of the two sides of a T account are compared and the debit amounts are more than the credits, an account has a debit balance. When the credits are more than the debits, the account has a credit balance.

Debit and Credit Procedure
In a **double-entry system**, each transaction is recorded in the appropriate account with at least one debit and at least one credit. Double-entry accounting ensures that total debits will always equal total credits.

This system is used all over the world and gives a logical method for recording transactions. Therefore, if the sum of the debits does not equal the sum of the credits an error has been made.

Assets and Liabilities
Recall the accounting equation: **assets = liabilities + owner's equity**. Assets are on the left side of the equation, so to be consistent, when the double-entry system was created, it was decided that the normal balance of the asset accounts should also be on the left side, which is a debit. Consequently, assets are increased by debits and decreased by credits.

Liabilities are on the right side of the accounting equation, thus the normal balance of a liability account would be on the right side—a credit. Thus, liabilities are increased by credits and decreased by debits.

Normal Account Balances
Debit (left)	**Credit (right)**
Assets	Liabilities
	Owner's Equity

Owner's Equity
Owner's Equity is the owner's claim to the assets of the business. It is increased by owner investment and revenues and decreased by owner's drawings and expenses. It is on the right side of the accounting equation and so the normal balance is a credit.

The owner's capital is the equity account of the sole owner of a business. Investments by the owner are credited to the owner's capital account. Similar to liabilities, owner's capital is increased by credits and decreased by debits.

Owner's Drawings are recorded in a separate general ledger account and represent withdrawal of cash or other assets by the owner for personal use. Drawings decrease owner's equity and have a normal debit balance. Consequently, drawings are increased by debits and decreased by credits.

Net Income results when revenues are greater than expenses. Revenues increase owner's equity and expenses decrease owner's equity. Revenue accounts are increased by credits and decreased by debits. Expense accounts are increased by debits and decreased by credits.

Normal Account Balances
Debit (left)	**Credit (right)**
Expenses	Revenues

Expanding the Basic Accounting Equation

The expanded basic accounting equation is:
Assets = Liabilities + Owner's Capital – Owner's Drawings + Revenues – Expenses

Debits / Credits and Normal Account Balances

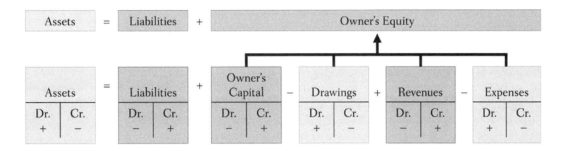

The normal balance of each account is on its increase side.

Steps in the Recording Process

study objective 2

Describe the basic steps in the recording process, explain what a journal is, and journalize business transactions.

The basic steps in the recording process are as follows:
1. Analyze each transaction for its effect on the accounts.
2. Enter the transaction information in a journal.
3 Transfer the journal information to the appropriate accounts in the ledger.

The basic steps in the recording process are repeated whether using a computerized or manual accounting system.

The Journal

Transactions are first recorded in a journal in date order. The journal is referred to as the book of original entry. The transactions are transferred to the accounts from the journal. The most basic form of journal is the **general journal.**

The journal is important to the recording process for the following reasons:
- It discloses, in one place, the complete effect of a transaction.
- It provides a date order record of transactions.
- It helps to prevent or locate errors because the debit and credit amounts for each entry can be readily compared.
- It gives an explanation of the transaction and identifies the source document if there is one.

Journalizing
Entering transaction data in the journal is known as journalizing. A complete entry consists of the following:
- the date of the transaction,
- the accounts and amounts to be debited and credited, and
- a brief explanation of the transaction.

In manual accounting and in computerized accounting, the format of the journals may be different but they serve the same purpose and the content is almost the same. Regardless of the type of accounting system used, the accounting equation must always be in balance.

If an entry affects only two accounts—one debit and one credit entry—it is a **simple journal entry**. If the entry affects three or more accounts, it is a **compound journal entry**. It is important to use correct and specific account titles when journalizing.

The Ledger

study objective 3

Explain what a ledger is and post journal entries.

The ledger is the entire group of accounts maintained by a company. It keeps, in one place, all the information about changes in account balances and is a useful source of data for management. For example, the Cash account in the ledger would show all additions and deductions from Cash for the period. It would not reveal information about any other account in the ledger. Any reference to the "ledger" means the general ledger.

Standard Form of Account
The standard form of a ledger account has three money columns—debit, credit, and balance columns. The balance of the account is determined after each transaction. There is an explanation column, which is usually left blank in manual accounting. In computerized accounting, explanations may be included because of the way the computer program is written.

Posting

Posting is the procedure of transferring journal entries to the ledger accounts. The following steps are used in posting:

1. **General Ledger**. Enter the date, journal page, and debit or credit amount shown in the journal.
2. **General Journal**. In the reference column of the journal, write the account numbers to which the debit and credit amounts were posted.

Posting should be done in chronological (date) order and on a timely basis to ensure that the ledger is up to date. All debits and credits of one journal entry should be posted one journal entry at a time.

In a computerized accounting system, posting usually occurs automatically right after each journal is entered.

The Chart of Accounts

A chart of accounts is a listing of accounts with numbers that identify their location in the ledger. Whether manual or computerized, the chart of accounts is designed as the framework for the entire database of accounting information. The numbering system starts with the balance sheet accounts, followed by the income statement accounts.

The chart of accounts for Pioneer Advertising Agency follows. Note that there are gaps in the numbering systems. This makes it possible to insert new accounts when and where they are needed without having to renumber the entire chart of accounts

PIONEER ADVERTISING AGENCY
Chart of Accounts

Assets		Owner's Equity	
101.	Cash	301.	C. Byrd, Capital
112.	Accounts Receivable	306.	C. Byrd, Drawings
129.	Advertising Supplies	350.	Income Summary
130.	Prepaid Insurance		
151.	Office Equipment	**Revenues**	
152.	Accumulated Amortization—Office Equipment	400.	Service Revenue
		Expenses	
Liabilities		611.	Advertising Supplies Expense
200.	Notes Payable	711.	Amortization Expense
201.	Accounts Payable	722.	Insurance Expense
209.	Unearned Revenue	726.	Salaries Expense
212.	Salaries Payable	729.	Rent Expense
230.	Interest Payable	905.	Interest Expense

The Recording Process

Before each transaction is journalized and posted, a basic analysis and a debit/credit analysis must be done. The basic steps in the recording process are illustrated as follows:

Transaction	On September 4, Fester Company pays $3,000 cash to a creditor in full payment of the balance due.
Basic Analysis	Accounts Payable decreases by $3,000 and Cash decreases by $3,000.
Debit/Credit Analysis	Debits decrease liabilities: debit Accounts Payable $3,000 Credits decrease Cash: credit Cash $3,000. Accounts Payable decreases by $3,000 and Cash decreases by $3,000.

Journal Entry	Sept 4	Accounts Payable	201	3,000	
		Cash	101		3,000
		Paid creditor			
		in full			

Posting

Cash	101		Accounts Payable	201
	Sept 4 3,000		Sept 4 3,000	

The Trial Balance

study objective 4

Explain the purpose of a trial balance and prepare one.

A trial balance is a **list of accounts and their balances** at a specific time. The main purpose of the trial balance is to prove (check) that total debits equal total credits after posting.

To prepare a trial balance:
1. List the account titles and their balances in the same order as the chart of accounts, with debit balances in the debit column and credit balances in the credit column.
2. Total the debit and credit columns.
3. Ensure the two columns are equal.

> **TIP**
> Try to get into the habit of listing the accounts on the trial balance in order of the accounting equation. This will reinforce your identification of assets, liabilities, equity, revenues, and expenses and will assist in financial statement preparation.

Limitations of a Trial Balance

A trial balance does not prove that all transactions have been recorded or that the ledger balances are correct. As long as an equal credit is posted when a debit amount is posted, the trial balance will balance. There may be several errors even when the trial balance columns agree.

Locating Errors

Locating errors in a manual accounting system can be time consuming. In a computerized accounting system, posting occurs when the journal entry is prepared and entered. This system lessens the chance of errors. Errors in a computerized system usually happen in the initial entry.

When manual trial balances do not balance, some of the errors may be (1) adding incorrect balances in the calculation of the account balances, (2) posting both sides of the entry as debits (or as credits), (3) transposing—when two numbers are reversed (for example, a debit of $325 is posted as $235), or (4) posting only half of the entry.

TIP

Much time and frustration can be avoided by carefully checking each journal entry as it is posted. Ensure that the entry has been posted exactly as it is recorded. Taking the extra time to review each journal entry as it is posted will eliminate most of the errors that would otherwise occur.

Simplistic Assumptions

Use of Dollars and Cents

Cents have been omitted in all of the illustrations and examples in the text and in this study guide. However, cents are included in the real world and are used in the business environment. Dollar signs are used only in the trial balance and in financial statements. Even when dollar signs are used, the use is limited, making financial reports easier to read.

Sales Taxes

Sales taxes are not included in the illustrations and examples in the text and in this study guide, even though they occur in the real world.

Demonstration Problem (SO 2, 3 and 4)

Doug Stein, the owner of Stein Accounting Agency, had the following transactions occur during January 2008:

Jan. 2   D. Stein begins business with a cash investment of $222,000.

6   Buys an office building for $120,000 cash. The building was valued at $50,000 and the land at $70,000.

10   Hires Pat Delaney as his assistant.

14   Performs consulting services for Simon Company worth $10,000, but is not paid at this time.

15   Receives $15,000 cash from Adeline Watters for services to be performed in March 2008.

17   Purchases supplies for $500 on credit.

20   Receives a $10,000 cheque from Simon Company.

28   Pays Pat Delaney $2,000 in salary for January.

30   Withdraws $3,000 for personal use to vacation in Jamaica.

31   Receives a $150 telephone bill for telephone service for January that must be paid by February 15.

The chart of accounts for Stein Accounting Agency is as follows:

Stein Accounting Agency
Chart of Accounts

	Assets		**Owner's Equity**
101	Cash	301	D. Stein, Capital
112	Accounts Receivable	305	D. Stein, Drawings
128	Accounting Supplies	351	Income Summary
130	Prepaid Insurance		
140	Land		**Revenues**
145	Office Building	401	Accounting Revenue
146	Accumulated Amortization—		
	Office Building		**Expenses**
151	Office Equipment	511	Accounting Supplies Expense
152	Accumulated Amortization—	611	Amortization Expense
	Office Equipment	622	Insurance Expense
		729	Rent Expense
	Liabilities	739	Salaries Expense
200	Notes Payable	905	Interest Expense
201	Accounts Payable	909	Telephone Expense
209	Unearned Revenue		
212	Salaries Payable		
230	Interest Payable		

Instructions

(a) Journalize the January transactions.
(b) Open ledger accounts and post the January transactions.
(c) Prepare a trial balance at January 31, 2008.

Solution to Demonstration Problem

(a)

General Journal				J1
Date	**Account Titles and Explanation**	**Ref**	**Debit**	**Credit**
Jan. 2	Cash	101	222,000	
	D. Stein, Capital	301		222,000
	Investment in business.			
6	Office Building	145	50,000	
	Land	140	70,000	
	Cash	101		120,000
	Purchase of office building.			
10	No journal entry; not a transaction.			
14	Accounts Receivable	112	10,000	
	Accounting Revenue	401		10,000
	Services performed for Simon Company.			
15	Cash	101	15,000	
	Unearned Revenue	209		15,000
	Received cash in advance from customer.			
17	Accounting Supplies	128	500	
	Accounts Payable	201		500
	Purchased supplies on account.			
20	Cash	101	10,000	
	Accounts Receivable	112		10,000
	Received $10,000 from Simon Company.			
28	Salaries Expense	739	2,000	
	Cash	101		2,000
	Paid Delaney for his wages earned.			
30	D. Stein, Drawings	305	3,000	
	Cash	101		3,000
	Withdraw cash for personal use			
31	Telephone Expense	909	150	
	Accounts Payable	201		150
	Recording expense to be paid in February.			

(b)

GENERAL LEDGER

Cash			101
Jan. 2	222,000	Jan. 6	120,000
15	15,000	3	2,000
20	10,000	20	3,000
Bal.	122,000		

Accounts receivable			112
Jan. 14	10,000	Jan. 20	10,000
Bal.	0		

Accounting Supplies			128
Jan. 17	500		
Bal.	500		

Land			140
Jan. 6	70,000		
Bal.	70,000		

Office Building			145
Jan. 6	50,000		
Bal.	50,000		

Accounts Payable			201
		Jan. 17	500
		31	150
		Bal.	650

Unearned Revenue			209
		Jan. 15	15,000
		Bal.	15,000

D. Stein, Capital			301
		Jan. 2	222,000
		Bal.	222,000

D. Stein, Drawings			305
		Jan. 30	3,000
		Bal.	3,000

Accounting Revenue			401
		Jan. 14	10,000
		Bal.	10,000

Salaries Expense			739
Jan. 28	2,000	Oct. 21	10,000
Bal.	2,000	Bal.	10,000

Telephone Expense			909
Jan. 31	150		
Bal.	150		

(c)

Stein Accounting Agency
Trial Balance
January 31, 2008

	Debit	Credit
Cash	$122,000	
Accounting supplies	500	
Land	70,000	
Building	50,000	
Accounts payable		$ 650
Unearned revenue		15,000
D. Stein, drawings	3,000	
D. Stein, capital		222,000
Accounting revenue		10,000
Salaries expense	2,000	
Telephone expense	150	
Totals	$247,650	$247,650

Review Questions and Exercises

Multiple Choice

Circle the letter that best answers each of the following statements.

1. (SO 1) An account is an individual accounting record of increases and decreases in specific:

    a. liabilities.
    b. assets.
    c. expenses.
    d. assets, liabilities, and owner's equity items.

2. (SO 1) The T account:

    a. can be found within the accounting records.
    b. has debit, credit, and balance columns.
    c. is used for illustration purposes.
    d. is used to record journal entries.

3. (SO 1) Credits:

    a. increase both assets and liabilities.
    b. decrease both assets and liabilities.
    c. increase assets and decrease liabilities.
    d. decrease assets and increase liabilities.

4. (SO 1) An account that is increased by a credit is:

    a. an asset account.
    b. a liability account.
    c. a drawings account.
    d. an expense account.

5. (SO 1) Which of the following rules is incorrect?

    a. Credits decrease the drawings account.
    b. Debits increase the capital account.
    c. Credits increase revenue accounts.
    d. Debits decrease liability accounts.

6. (SO 1) An account that is increased by a debit is a:

    a. liability account.
    b. drawings account.
    c. capital account.
    d. revenue account.

7. (SO 1) An account that is increased by a credit is a(n):

    a. drawings account.
    b. revenue account.
    c. expense account.
    d. asset account.

8. (SO 2) Which of the following is the correct sequence of steps in the recording process?

    a. Posting, journalizing, analyzing.
    b. Journalizing, analyzing, posting.
    c. Analyzing, posting, journalizing.
    d. Analyzing, journalizing, posting.

9. (SO 2) The column in the general journal that is not used during journalizing is the:

    a. date column.
    b. account title column.
    c. reference column.
    d. debit amount column.

10. (SO 2) Which of the following is a false statement?

    a. The account Service Revenue is increased with a credit.
    b. A compound entry is when two or more accounts are affected in one journal entry.
    c. Owner's Drawings is increased by a debit entry.
    d. All transactions are initially recorded in a journal.

11. (SO 2) Which of the following is not considered a significant contribution of the journal to the recording process?

    a. The journal provides a chronological record of all transactions.
    b. The journal provides a means of accumulating, in one place, all the information about changes in account balances.
    c. The journal discloses, in one place, the complete effect of a transaction.
    d. The journal helps prevent or locate errors since the debit and credit amounts for each entry can be readily compared.

12. (SO 2) On March 13, 2008, McClory Company purchases equipment for $900 and supplies for $300 from Rudnicky Company for $1,200 cash. The entry for this transaction will include a:

    a. debit to Equipment $900 and a debit to Supplies Expense $300 for Rudnicky.
    b. credit to Cash for Rudnicky.
    c. credit to Accounts Payable for McClory.
    d. debit to Equipment $900 and a debit to Supplies $300 for McClory.

13. (SO 2) Laventhol Company sells $300 of equipment to Reiner Company on credit. Reiner will enter the transaction in the journal with a:

    a. debit to Accounts Receivable and a credit to Sales.
    b. debit to Accounts Receivable and a credit to Equipment.
    c. credit to Accounts Payable and a debit to Equipment.
    d. credit to Cash and a debit to Equipment.

14. (SO 2) Szykowny Co. buys a machine from Scott Company, paying half in cash and putting the balance on account. The journal entry for this transaction by Szykowny will include a:

    a. credit to Accounts Payable and a credit to Cash.
    b. credit to Notes Payable and a credit to Cash.
    c. debit to Supplies and a credit to Cash.
    d. debit to Machinery and a credit to Notes Payable.

15. (SO 2) Hrubec Company pays $1,800 cash for a one-year insurance policy on July 1, 2008. The policy will expire on June 30, 2009. The entry on July 1, 2008, is:

    a. debit Insurance Expense $1,800; credit Cash $1,800.
    b. debit Prepaid Insurance $1,800; credit Cash $1,800.
    c. debit Insurance Expense $1,800; credit Accounts Payable $1,800.
    d. debit Prepaid Insurance $1,800; credit Accounts Payable $1,800.

16. (SO 2) Kevin Walsh withdraws $300 cash from his business for personal use. The entry for this transaction will include a debit of $300 to:

    a. K. Walsh, Drawings.
    b. K. Walsh, Capital.
    c. Drawings Expense.
    d. Salaries Expense.

17. (SO 2) Vicki Wagner Dance Studio bills a client for dancing lessons given during the past week. The journal entry will include a credit to:

    a. V. Wagner, Capital.
    b. Unearned Dance Revenue.
    c. Dance Revenue.
    d. Accounts Receivable.

18. (SO 2) Golden Pork Company receives $400 from a customer on October 15 in payment of balance due for services billed on October 1. The entry by Golden Pork Company will include a credit of $400 to:

    a. Notes Receivable.
    b. Service Revenue.
    c. Accounts Receivable.
    d. Unearned Service Revenue.

19. (SO 2) On October 3, Mike Baker, a carpenter, received a cash payment for services previously billed to a client. Mike paid his telephone bill, and he also bought equipment on credit. For the three transactions, at least one of the entries will include a:

    a. credit to M. Baker, Capital.
    b. credit to Notes Payable.
    c. debit to Accounts Receivable.
    d. credit to Accounts Payable.

20. (SO 3) The chart of accounts is a:

    a. list of accounts and their balances at a specific time.
    b. device used to prove the mathematical accuracy of the ledger.
    c. listing of the accounts and the account numbers that identify their location in the ledger.
    d. required step in the recording process.

21. (SO 3) The process of posting in a manual system is not complete until:

    a. each journal entry is correctly balanced.
    b. the amounts posted from the journal are correct.
    c. the posting reference column in the journal is cross-referenced to the ledger.
    d. the post-closing trial balance is prepared.

22. (SO 3, 4) The South Forks Company posted a journal entry recording the collection of a $1,248 account receivable as a debit to the Cash general ledger account in the amount of $1,248 and a credit to the Accounts Receivable general ledger account in the amount of $1,428. The following needs to occur to correct the posting error:

    a. The Cash general ledger account debit posting should be changed from $1,248 to $1,428.
    b. A one-sided journal entry should be made and posted debiting the Cash general ledger account for $180.
    c. The Accounts Receivable general ledger account posting should be changed from $1,428 to $1,248.
    d. No correction is necessary because the general journal was recorded properly.

23. (SO 4) The main purpose of the trial balance is to:

    a. check that the posting from the journal is correct.
    b. check that the debits equal the credits after posting.
    c. make sure that principles and assumptions have been correctly followed.
    d. determine that the company is making a profit.

24. (SO 4) The trial balance will balance in all cases except when:

    a. a journal entry has been posted to incorrect accounts.
    b. one side of the journal entry has not been posted.
    c. both sides of the journal entry have been posted with transposed numbers.
    d. the transaction has not been posted.

25. (SO 4) A trial balance will not balance if:

    a. a journal entry is posted twice.
    b. a wrong amount is used in journalizing.
    c. incorrect account titles are used in journalizing.
    d. a journal entry is only partially posted.

Matching

Match each term with its definition by writing the appropriate letter in the space provided.

Terms	**Definitions**
____ 1. Account	a. The entire group of accounts maintained by a company.
____ 2. T account	b. A list of accounts and the account numbers that identify their location in the ledger.
____ 3. Posting	c. An individual accounting record of increases and decreases in a specific asset, liability, or owner's equity item.
____ 4. Trial balance	d. The right side of an account.
____ 5. Debit	e. The left side of an account.
____ 6. Credit	f. The procedure of transferring journal entries to the ledger accounts.
____ 7. Chart of accounts	g. A system that records the dual effect of each transaction in appropriate accounts.
____ 8. Ledger	h. The form of an account with a title and a left or debit side and a right or credit side.
____ 9. Journalizing	i. An accounting record in which transactions are initially recorded in chronological order.
____ 10. Journal	j. The procedure of entering transaction data in the journal.
____ 11. Double-entry system	k. A list of accounts and their balances at a given time.

Exercises

E2-1   (SO 1) The ledger of the Gilbert Company includes the accounts listed below.

Instructions

For each account indicate: (a) whether it is an asset, liability, or owner's equity item, (b) its normal balance, and (c) the statement in which it would appear. Use the following format for your answer. The Cash account is given as an example.

Account	(a) Type of Account	(b) Normal Balance	(c) Financial Statement
Cash	Asset	Debit	Balance Sheet
Equipment	_____	_____	_____
Wages Payable	_____	_____	_____
Telephone Expense	_____	_____	_____
Notes Receivable	_____	_____	_____
Commission Revenue	_____	_____	_____
J. Gilbert, Capital	_____	_____	_____
Rent Expense	_____	_____	_____
Supplies	_____	_____	_____
J. Gilbert, Drawings	_____	_____	_____
Service Revenue	_____	_____	_____

E2-2   (SO 2) Sean Winston, the ship captain and president of Winston Ship Lines, had the following transactions occur during the month of February 2008:

Feb.   3   Paid $1,000 to Jack Edwards, the ship's bursar, for wages earned in January. These wages were expensed in January.

7   Received $35,000 cash from R.J. Hughes for a cruise taken by R.J. and his family last month. This revenue was properly recorded last month.

11   Purchased equipment from Durham Inc. for $50,000 on credit.

20   Received $25,000 cash from Ron Southern upon completion of a cruise taken by Ron and his friends this month. (Credit Cruise Revenue)

26   Received $31,000 cash from J. Zimmerman for a cruise to be taken next month.

28   Paid $20,000 cash to McGraw Insurance Company for a 6-month insurance policy to expire August 31.

Instructions
Record the transactions in the journal provided below.

	General Journal		J1
Date	**Account Titles and Explanation**	**Debit**	**Credit**
2008			

E2-3   (SO 4) The ledger for Thorson Advertising Agency at October 31, 2008, contains the following data. Assume that all accounts have normal balances.

Accounts Payable	$7,500
Accounts Receivable	9,500
Cash	?
Commission Revenue	7,000
P. Thorson, Capital	10,500
P. Thorson, Drawings	500
Rent Expense	900
Salaries Expense	4,060
Supplies	600
Unearned Commission Revenue	1,200

Instructions

Prepare a trial balance at October 31, 2008.

THORSON ADVERTISING AGENCY
Trial Balance
October 31, 2008

	Debit	Credit

E2-4 (SO 4) The following trial balance is not balanced because of errors. Identify the errors that have occurred. Hint: Check the normal balances of the account, then use techniques described in the text to find other errors.

Caryl's Events Agency
Trial Balance
July 31, 2008

	Debit	Credit
Cash	$25,800	
Accounts receivable	2,100	
Prepaid insurance	5,300	
Notes payable	17,900	
Accounts payable		$ 3,200
Unearned revenue		3,300
L. Dean, capital		10,000
L. Dean, drawings	1,000	
Events revenue		40,000
Salaries expense	36,000	
Rent expense	5,200	
Telephone expense	800	
Totals	$94,100	$56,500

E2-5 (SO 2) Cui Tu, a business woman from China, sent her accountant Melissa Vialva a cheque in the amount of $5,000 for work to be done in the year 2008. Ms. Vialva received the cheque on January 15, 2008. Ms. Vialva deposited the amount into her cash account and proceeded to do the work. The work was only half completed by March 31, 2008. On March 31, Ms. Vialva was preparing quarterly financial statements for her business.

Instructions
Explain the following:

(a) The entry that would have been made on January 15, 2008, which accounts were used, and why.

_____

_____

_____

(b) The entry required on March 31, and why it would be done.

_____

_____

_____

Solutions to Review Questions and Exercises

Multiple Choice

1. (d)   An account is an individual accounting record of increases and decreases in specific asset, liability, and owner's equity items.

2. (c)   The T account is used for illustration purposes. It is an excellent way to explain accounting relationships.

3. (d)   Credits decrease assets and increase liabilities.

4. (b)   An asset account (a), a drawings account (c), and an expense account (d) are all accounts that normally have a debit balance; thus, they are increased by debits.

5. (b)   Debits decrease the capital account because the capital account has a credit balance as its normal balance. Choices (a), (c), and (d) are all correct rules concerning increasing or decreasing accounts.

6. (b)   A liability account (a), a capital account (c), and a revenue account (d) are all accounts that normally have a credit balance; therefore, they are increased by a credit. The drawings account has a normal debit balance and will increase with a debit.

7. (b)   A drawings account (a), an expense account (c), and an asset account (d) are all accounts that normally have a debit balance. A revenue account has a normal credit balance and will increase with a credit entry.

8. (d)   The basic steps in the recording process are:
    1. Analyze each transaction.
    2. Enter the transaction information in a journal (journalizing).
    3. Post the journal information to the ledger.

9. (c)   The date column (a), the account title column (b), and the debit amount column (d) are all used during the journalizing procedure. The reference column is used later when the journal entries are posted to the ledger.

10. (b)   A compound entry is when three or more accounts are effected in one journal entry. Choices (a), (c), and (d) are all true statements.

11. (b)   The ledger—not the journal—provides a means of accumulating, in one place, all the information about changes in account balances. Answers (a), (c), and (d) are all considered significant contributions by the journal to the recording process.

12. (d)   McClory Company will make the following entry:

Mar. 13	Equipment	900	
	Supplies	300	
	Cash		1,200
	Purchase equipment and supplies for cash.		

13. (c) Reiner Company purchased from Laventhol Company on account, therefore (a) and (b) are incorrect. Cash was not involved in the transaction, therefore (d) is incorrect.

14. (a) The journal entry for this transaction is as follows:

Date	Equipment	XXXX	
	Accounts Payable		XXXX
	Cash		XXXX
	Purchase equipment for cash and on account.		

15. (b) The one-year policy will benefit more than one accounting period. Therefore, the entry is:

Jul. 1	Prepaid Insurance	900	
	Cash		900
	Purchase one-year insurance policy.		

(This answer is the best choice for this question even though it is not the only choice.)

16. (a) The withdrawal of cash and other assets by an owner for personal use is a drawings and not an expense. The entry is:

Date	Kevin Walsh, Drawings	300	
	Cash		300
	Withdraw cash for personal use.		

17. (c) The transaction is recorded in the journal as follows:

Date	Accounts Receivable	XXXX	
	Dance Revenue		XXXX
	Billed customer for services performed on account.		

18. (c) The entry by Golden Pork Company is:

Oct. 15	Cash	400	
	Accounts Receivable		400
	Payment received on account.		

19. (d) The three transactions are recorded in the journal as follows:

Oct. 3	Cash	XXXX	
	Accounts Receivable		XXXX
	Payment received on account.		

Oct. 3	Telephone Expense	XXXX	
	Cash		XXXX
	Payment of telephone bill.		

Oct. 3	Equipment	XXXX	
	Accounts Payable		XXXX
	Purchase of equipment on account.		

20. (c) The chart of accounts is a listing of accounts and the account numbers that identify their location in the ledger. Both answers (a) and (b) are characteristics of a trial balance. Answer (d) is incorrect because a chart of accounts is not required.

21. (c) The posting reference column in the journal is cross-referenced to the ledger and vice versa.

22. (c) The credit to Accounts Receivable is incorrect and needs to be corrected by changing the incorrect amount to the correct amount. Answer (b) is incorrect because there is no such thing as a one-sided entry.

23. (b) The trial balance only verifies mathematical correctness. When the total debits are equal to the total credits, the primary purpose of the trial balance has been achieved.

24. (b) The trial balance will balance when postings are incorrect as long as there are equal debits and credits posted to the ledger. So, if one side of an entry has not been posted, the trial balance will not balance.

25. (d) The trial balance may still balance even when a journal entry is posted twice (a), a wrong amount is used in journalizing (b), and incorrect account titles are used (c). A journal entry that is only partially posted means that a debit or credit posting is omitted; thus, the trial balance will not balance.

Matching

1.	c	5.	e	9.	j
2.	h	6.	d	10.	i
3.	f	7.	b	11.	g
4.	k	8.	a		

Exercises

E2-1

Account	(a) Type of Account	(b) Normal Balance	(c) Financial Statement
Equipment	Asset	Debit	Balance Sheet
Wages Payable	Liability	Credit	Balance Sheet
Telephone Expense	Owner's equity	Debit	Income Statement
Notes Receivable	Asset	Debit	Balance Sheet
Commission Revenue	Owner's equity	Credit	Owner's Equity
J. Gilbert, Capital	Owner's equity	Credit	Owner's Equity Balance Sheet
Rent Expense	Owner's equity	Debit	Income Statement
Supplies	Asset	Debit	Balance Sheet
J. Gilbert, Drawings	Owner's equity	Debit	Owner's Equity
Service Revenue	Owner's equity	Credit	Income Statement

E2-2

General Journal			J1	
Date	**Account Titles and Explanation**	**Debit**	**Credit**	
2008				
Feb. 3	Wages Payable	1,000		
	Cash		1,000	
	Paid wages earned.			
7	Cash	35,000		
	Accounts Receivable		35,000	
	Received payment from R.J. Hughes.			
11	Equipment	50,000		
	Accounts Payable		50,000	
	Purchased equipment from Durham on account.			
20	Cash	25,000		
	Cruise Revenue		25,000	
	Received payment from Ron Southern.			
26	Cash	31,000		
	Unearned Cruise Revenue		31,000	
	Received advance from J. Zimmerman for future cruise.			
28	Prepaid Insurance	20,000		
	Cash		20,000	
	Paid 6-month policy; effective date March 1.			

E2-3

	Debit	Credit
THORSON ADVERTISING AGENCY		
Trial Balance		
October 31, 2008		
Cash	$10,640	
Accounts receivable	9,500	
Supplies	600	
Accounts payable		$ 7,500
Unearned commission revenue		1,200
P. Thorson, capital		10,500
P. Thorson, drawings	500	
Commission revenue		7,000
Rent expense	900	
Salaries expense	4,060	
	$26,200	$26,200

E2-4

Error 1. A check of the normal balances shows that the balance in the note payable account is on the debit side of the trial balance.

Solution 1. Move $17,900 to the credit side of the trial balance.

Error 2. The trial balance now has a difference of $1,800. This difference is exactly divisible by 9. The product of the division is 300. Therefore, there must have been a transposition where the difference between two numbers transposed must be 2.

Solution 2. The only possibility is Prepaid Insurance. Correcting the Prepaid Insurance account from "5,300" to "3,500" causes the trial balance to balance.

CARYL'S EVENTS AGENCY
Trial Balance
July 31, 2008

	Debit	Credit
Cash	$25,800	
Accounts receivable	2,100	
Prepaid insurance	5,300	
Notes payable	17,900	
Accounts payable		$3,200
Unearned revenue		3,300
L. Dean, capital		10,000
L. Dean, drawings	1,000	
Events revenue		40,000
Salaries expense	36,000	
Rent expense	5,200	
Telephone expense	800	
Totals	$94,100	$56,500

E2-5

(a) The entry made would be a debit to Cash and a credit to Unearned Revenue. This would be necessary because Ms. Vialva has not yet earned the revenue—Ms. Tu paid her in advance. The Unearned Revenue account is a liability in Ms. Vialva's books.

(b) On March 31, Ms. Vialva would move $2,500 of the amount in the Unearned Revenue account (debit) to the Revenue Earned account (credit). This would record her earnings for the completed work ($5,000 x 1/2).

chapter 3
Adjusting the Accounts

study objectives >>

After studying this chapter, you should be able to:
1. Explain the time period assumption, revenue recognition principle, matching principle, and accrual basis of accounting.
2. Prepare adjusting entries for prepayments.
3. Prepare adjusting entries for accruals.
4. Describe the nature and purpose of an adjusted trial balance and prepare one.
5. Prepare adjusting entries for the alternative treatment of prepayments (Appendix 3A).

Preview of Chapter 3

In Chapter 2 we examined the recording process up to and including the preparation of the trial balance. Before financial statements can be prepared, additional steps are necessary to adjust for timing mismatches and to report revenues and expenses in the appropriate time period. This chapter is organized as follows:

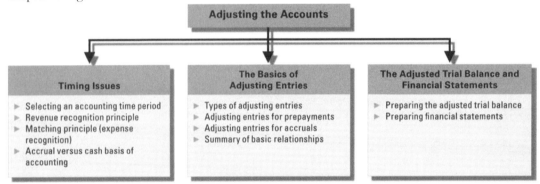

Timing Issues

If a company waited until it ended its operations to prepare financial statements, it would perhaps wait for 40 years from when the business first opened its doors to the date that the business ceased to exist. Business owners would never know how the business was operating from one period (perhaps a year) to the next. This is not practical.

Selecting an Accounting Time Period

study objective 1

Explain the time period assumption, revenue recognition principle, matching principle, and accrual basis of accounting.

Accountants have made the assumption that the economic life of a business can be divided into artificial time periods. This assumption is referred to as the time period assumption. Accounting time periods can be a month, a quarter, or one year. Time periods of less than one year are called interim periods.

The accounting period of one year in length is known as a fiscal year. Many businesses choose January 1 to December 31 (a calendar year) as their fiscal year. Others choose a date different from December 31 as their fiscal year end, to coincide with a time when business activity is slow.

Accountants have developed two generally accepted accounting principles to determine the amount of revenues and expenses to report in a specific accounting period. They are (1) the revenue recognition principle, and (2) the matching principle.

Revenue Recognition Principle

The revenue recognition principle states that revenue must be recognized in the accounting period in which it is earned. Note that the revenue earned may not necessarily be received in cash by the business during the same accounting period.

Matching Principle (Expense Recognition)

The matching principle states that efforts (expenses) must be matched with accomplishments (revenues). This principle requires a business to include all expenses in the same accounting period as the revenues it earns. In effect, expense recognition is tied to revenue recognition.

Accrual versus Cash Basis of Accounting

Under the accrual basis of accounting, transactions that change a company's financial statements are recorded in the periods in which the events occur. Accrual accounting follows the revenue recognition and matching principles and is in accordance with generally accepted accounting principles (GAAP).

Under the cash basis of accounting, revenue is recorded when cash is received and expenses are recorded when cash is paid. The cash basis of accounting often results in misleading financial statements and is not in accordance with GAAP.

The Basics of Adjusting Entries

Adjusting entries are required every time financial statements are prepared. Each account in the trial balance is analyzed to see if it is up to date. Analysis requires a thorough understanding of the company's operations.

Adjusting entries are made for the following reasons:

1. Some events are not journalized daily because it is not efficient to do so—for example, the consumption of supplies.

2. Some costs are not journalized during the accounting period because they expire with the passage of time rather than through daily transactions—for example, insurance premiums (the cost of the insurance policy) paid at the beginning of the period.

3. Some items may be unrecorded—for example, amounts owing for services obtained in the period being reported, but the bills will not be received until after the period is over.

Types of Adjusting Entries

Adjusting entries can be classified as prepayments (prepaid expenses or unearned revenue) or accruals (accrued revenues or accrued expenses).

Prepayments	Accruals
1. Prepaid Expenses Expenses paid in cash and recorded as assets before they are used or consumed.	1. Accrued Expenses Expenses incurred but not yet paid in cash or recorded.
2. Unearned Revenues Cash received and recorded as a liability before revenue is earned.	2. Accrued Revenues Revenues earned but not yet received in cash or recorded.

Each adjusting entry affects one balance sheet account and one income statement account.

> **TIP**
> The Cash account is never used in adjusting entries, except for bank reconciliations, which will be discussed in a later chapter.

Adjusting Entries for Prepayments

study objective 2

Prepare adjusting entries for prepayments.

Prepayments are either prepaid expenses or unearned revenues. Adjusting entries are used to record the portion of the prepayment that is for the expense incurred or the revenue earned in the current accounting period.

Prepaid Expenses

Prepaid expenses are costs paid in cash and recorded as assets before they are used or consumed. Prepaid expenses expire with the passage of time or as the asset is used up.

At each statement date, adjusting entries are made for two purposes: (1) to record the expenses that apply to the current accounting period, and (2) to show the unexpired costs in the asset accounts.

Supplies

When businesses buy supplies, the amount purchased is usually debited to an asset account. The amount of supplies used is only recorded during the adjustment process when a physical inventory of supplies is taken. When the inventory count is taken, the amount that remains is the amount of the asset—Supplies. An asset–expense account relationship exists with prepaid expenses for supplies.

Insurance

Most companies' insurance policies are normally charged to the asset account Prepaid Insurance. If no adjustment to the Prepaid Insurance account was ever made, assets would be overstated and expenses would be understated.

To illustrate a prepaid insurance adjusting entry, assume that on October 1 Kubitz Company pays $2,400 cash to Sandy Insurance Company for a one-year insurance policy, effective October 1. The entry to record the purchase of the insurance policy would be as follows:

Oct. 1	Prepaid Insurance	2,400	
	Cash		2,400

On the date of adjustment, October 31, the entry to record insurance expense for one month would be as follows:

Oct. 31	Insurance Expense	200	
	Prepaid Insurance		200
	Insurance expense for October: $2,400/12		

The adjusting entry results in a debit to an expense account and a credit to an asset account

Amortization

The purchase of a long-lived asset is basically a long-term prepayment for services. Similar to other prepaid expenses, it is necessary to recognize the related expense as the asset is being used up. Amortization is the allocation of the cost of the long-lived asset to the Amortization Expense account over the asset's useful life. Land is not amortized as it has an unlimited useful life.

Calculation of Amortization

A common method of calculating amortization expense is dividing the cost of the asset by its useful life in years. This is called the straight-line amortization method.

Cost of asset ÷ years of useful life = amortization expense (annual)

The useful life of the asset must be estimated; thus, amortization is an estimate rather than an actual measurement. For periods less than a year, the annual expense amount must be adjusted for the relevant portion pertaining to that year.

In recording amortization, Amortization Expense is debited, so the expense increases. The asset, which is in effect a prepayment, is being used up and is in fact decreasing. However, it is important to keep track of the original cost of long-lived assets as well as to record the portion being used up over time. An account called Accumulated Amortization is credited with the amount used up. This account is called a contra asset account, and the portion of the asset that is used up is recorded in that account over the useful life of the asset.

To illustrate an adjusting entry for amortization, assume that Resch Company purchases a machine that has a useful life of five years for $6,000 cash on January 1, 2008. The annual amortization under the straight-line method is $6,000 ÷ 5 years = $1,200 per year. The adjusting entry for 2008 is:

Dec. 31	Amortization Expense	1,200	
	Accumulated Amortization—Machinery		1,200
	To record annual amortization for 2008		

Statement Presentation

Accumulated Amortization—Machinery is deducted from the Machinery account on the balance sheet. The difference between the cost of any amortizable asset and its accumulated amortization is referred to as the net book value of that asset.

Machinery	$6,000
Accumulated Amortization—Machinery	1,200
Net book value	$4,800

The net book value does not represent the market value of the asset. The net book value is the unallocated cost.

TIP

For assets that are bought on a specific date and consumed over time (e.g., insurance and amortizable assets), follow these steps to determine what amounts to input on the financial statements:

1. Draw a timeline to determine the amount of prepaid expense that has been consumed during the period.
2. The timeline should indicate the dates that the coverage began and the date it ends, or the date the asset was purchased and the years of its useful life.
3. Mark the timeline at the date you wish to prepare financial statements and count the number of months that have expired since the coverage began or the amortizable asset was purchased.
4. The period between when the coverage began or the asset was purchased and the financial statement date represents the expense that will be reported on the income statement.
5. The remainder of the timeline represents the amount of the asset (prepaid expense) that will be reported on the balance sheet.
6. The cost of long-lived assets would be reported at historical cost minus the accumulated amortization as the asset's net book value.

Unearned Revenues

When cash is received before it is earned as revenue, it is recorded as a liability to reflect the claim on the business to deliver services in the future. (Should the service not be performed, the cash would not be earned; it would have to be refunded to the customer). Therefore, unearned revenue is a liability and not a revenue account. Examples of unearned revenues include rent, magazine subscriptions, and customer deposits for future service.

Unearned revenues are subsequently earned when a service is provided to a customer. The adjusting entry results in a debit to a liability account and a credit to a revenue account. Prior to adjustment, liabilities are overstated and revenues are understated. It is not practical to make daily journal entries as revenue is earned. Instead, recognition of the earned revenue is delayed until the end of the accounting period.

To illustrate an unearned revenue adjusting entry, assume that on October 1 Schoen Company receives $3,000 cash from a tenant in payment of monthly rent for the period October through December. The entry to record the receipt of cash would be as follows:

| Oct. 1 | Cash | 3,000 | |
| | Unearned Rent Revenue | | 3,000 |

The adjusting entry to record the rent earned in October is:

Oct. 31	Unearned Rent Revenue	1,000	
	Rent Revenue		1,000
	To record rent earned in October: $3,000 \div 3$		

After the adjustment is made, $2,000 (rent for November and December) remains as a liability in the Unearned Rent Revenue account of Schoen Company.

Adjusting Entries for Accruals

study objective 3

Prepare adjusting entries for accruals.

Accruals refer to revenue and expense items that are not recognized through daily entries and are not recorded in the accounts. However, the revenue has been earned and the expense incurred by the company. They are unlike prepayments because they have not already been entered in the accounts. In the case of accruals, cash has not yet been received (accrued revenue) or paid (accrued expense). Since cash has not been received or paid, it is unlikely that there would be any entries in the accounts relating to the revenue or expense to be accrued. In other words, there is no original entry with an accrual like there is with a prepayment.

Accrued Revenues

Accrued revenues are revenues earned but not yet received in cash or recorded in the revenue account at the date of the statement. Accrued revenues are in effect the opposite of unearned revenues. In the case of accrued revenue, cash has not been received yet; in the case of unearned revenues, cash is received in advance.

An adjusting entry is required to record accrued revenue for two reasons: (1) to show the amount of revenue receivable at the balance sheet date, and (2) to record the revenue that has been earned during the period. Before the adjustment, both assets and revenues are understated.

To illustrate an accrued revenue adjusting entry, assume that in October Dr. Mayer, a dentist, performs $800 of services for patients who will not be billed until November. The adjusting entry for October is:

Oct. 31   Accounts Receivable   800
                                 Dental Fees Earned   800
                           To record dental fees earned in October

Accrued Expenses

Accrued expenses are expenses not yet paid or recorded at the statement date. Accrued expenses accumulate just as accrued revenues do. Accrued expenses include interest, rent, and salaries. Adjustments for accrued expenses are made for two reasons: (1) to record the amounts that are owed as of the balance sheet date, and (2) to record the expenses that apply to the current accounting period.

The adjusting entry for accrued expenses results in an increase (debit) to an expense account and an increase (credit) to a liability account.

Accrued Interest

Accrued interest occurs when a company owes interest on money borrowed and the interest is not due or has not been paid at the statement date. The formula for the calculation of interest is as follows:

$$\begin{matrix} \text{Face Value} \\ \text{of Note} \end{matrix} \quad \text{x} \quad \begin{matrix} \text{Annual Interest} \\ \text{Rate} \end{matrix} \quad \text{x} \quad \begin{matrix} \text{Time in Terms} \\ \text{of One Year} \end{matrix} \quad = \quad \text{Interest}$$

To illustrate an accrued interest adjusting entry, assume that on April 1 Deerling Company has signed a $6,000, six-month, 5% note payable that will be due on September 30. The total interest due on September 30 will be $150 ($6,000 x 5% x 6/12). Deerling prepares adjusting entries annually at the end of the fiscal year on May 31. The adjusting entry is:

May 31   Interest Expense   50
                                 Interest Payable   50
                           To record accrued interest expense: $6,000 x 5% x 2/12

On September 30, when the note becomes due, Deerling will record $100 ($6,000 x 5% x 4/12) of interest expense for the final four months of the note in the following entry:

Sep. 30   Interest Expense   100
                                 Note Payable   6,000
                                 Interest Payable   50
                                 Cash   6,150
                           To record payment of the note and interest

Accrued Salaries

Accrued salaries are salaries that will be paid to employees after work has been performed. In the employer's records, salaries (expense) would be understated and the employees claim to their salaries (liabilities) would be understated if an adjusting entry was not made.

To illustrate an accrued salaries adjusting entry, assume that Schwenk Company incurs salaries of $4,000 during the last week of October, which will be paid in November. The adjusting entry for October is:

Oct. 31   Salaries Expense   4,000
                                 Salaries Payable   4,000
                           To record accrued salaries

If Schwenk pays salaries of $5,500 on November 3, this includes $4,000 for salaries accrued to October 31 and $1,500 of salaries earned in November. The entry to record the payment of salaries on November 3 is:

Nov. 3	Salaries Expense	1,500	
	Salaries Payable		4,000
	Cash		6,000
	To record November 3 payroll		

Summary of Basic Relationships

	Type of Adjustment	Reason for Adjustment	Accounts before Adjustment	Adjusting Entry
Prepayments	Prepaid expenses	Prepaid expenses, originally recorded in asset accounts, have been used.	Assets overstated; expenses understated	Dr. Expense Cr. Asset
	Unearned revenues	Unearned revenues, originally recorded in liability accounts, have been earned.	Liabilities overstated; revenues understated	Dr. Liability Cr. Revenue
Accruals	Accrued revenues	Revenues have been earned but not yet received in cash or recorded.	Assets understated; revenues understated	Dr. Asset Cr. Revenue
	Accrued expenses	Expenses have been incurred but not yet paid in cash or recorded.	Expenses understated; liabilities understated	Dr. Expense Cr. Liability

The Adjusted Trial Balance and Financial Statements

After all adjusting entries have been journalized and posted, an adjusted trial balance is prepared. This trial balance shows the balances of all accounts, including those that have been adjusted, at the end of the accounting period.

Preparing the Adjusted Trial Balance

study objective 4

Describe the nature and purpose of an adjusted trial balance and prepare one.

An adjusted trial balance proves that total debit balances are equal to total credit balances in the ledger after all adjustments have been made. Financial statements can be prepared directly from the adjusted trial balance since all relevant revenue and expenses have been recorded. Financial statements cannot be prepared if the trial balance does not balance because the accounting equation (assets = liabilities + owner's equity) would not be in balance.

TIP

To differentiate between an unadjusted and an adjusted trial balance, check to see if any amortization expense has been claimed for the period. Any business that has long-term assets, such as buildings and equipment, must expense a portion of the cost of these assets as amortization expense before preparing financial statements. Compare Illustration 3-3 to Illustration 3-6 in the text.

Preparing Financial Statements

Financial statements can be prepared directly from the adjusted trial balance. The illustration of Pioneer Advertising Agency in Illustrations 3-7 and 3-8 in the text shows the interrelationship of the data.

The income statement is prepared from the adjusted balances of the revenue and expense accounts. The statement of owner's equity is prepared from the owner's capital and drawings and from the net income (or net loss) shown in the income statement. The balance sheet is then prepared from the asset and liability accounts and the ending owner's capital reported in the statement of owner's equity.

Appendix 3A

Alternative Treatment of Prepaid Expenses and Unearned Revenues

Some businesses record prepaid expenses and unearned revenues as expense and revenue, respectively, when cash is paid or received. This alternative treatment is acceptable for businesses that use it. However, different adjusting entries are needed on the financial statement date.

> **study objective 5**
>
> Prepare adjusting entries for the alternative treatment of prepayments (Appendix 3A).

Prepaid Expenses

When a business uses the alternative method to record prepaid expenses, the full amount of the cash payment is debited to expense. The business expects to consume all of the prepaid item before the next financial statement date. To adjust a prepaid item under the alternative method, it is necessary to calculate the amount of the cost that has not been used in the statement period and record this amount as an asset.

To illustrate, assume Reba Company has recorded all store supplies purchased over the period in the Store Supplies Expense account, which has a debit balance of $3,000. On the statement date, December 31, the store's supplies inventory is $1,000. The adjusting entry is as follows:

Dec. 31	Store Supplies	1,000	
	Store Supplies Expense		1,000
	To record store supplies inventory		

Since only $2,000 of store supplies have been used up, the expense account needs to be reduced by $1,000. An adjusting entry under the alternative treatment of prepaid expenses will always involve a debit to an asset account and a credit to an expense account.

Unearned Revenues

When a business uses the alternative method to record unearned revenue, the full amount of the cash received is credited to revenue. No liability is set up to recognize the claim on the business to deliver goods and services in the future. To adjust a prepaid revenue item under the alternative method, it is necessary to calculate the amount of the revenue that has not been earned and record this amount as a liability.

To illustrate, assume Tanner Company deposited all cash received during the period in the Service Revenue account. On the statement date, December 31, the balance in the revenue account is $30,000. However, analysis shows that $6,500 of the revenue has not been earned. The entry to adjust the revenue account is as follows:

Dec. 31   Service Revenue   6,500
                       Unearned Revenue   6,500
                 To record unearned revenue

In effect, $23,500 ($30,000 − $6,500) has been earned during the period reported by Tanner Company. An adjusting entry under the alternative treatment of revenue prepaid by customers will always involve a debit to a revenue account and a credit to a liability account.

Demonstration Problem (SO 2 and 3)

At December 31, 2008, the unadjusted trial balance of Thresher Company shows the following balances for selected accounts:

Supplies	$ 8,500
Prepaid Insurance	12,000
Equipment	40,000
Accumulated Amortization—Equipment	16,000
Unearned Revenue	15,000
Notes Payable	50,000
Service Revenue	40,000

Analysis reveals the following additional data pertaining to these accounts:
1. Supplies on hand at December 31, 2008, is $3,000.
2. Insurance coverage began on June 1, 2008, for a one-year policy.
3. The equipment was purchased January 1, 2008, and was estimated to have a useful life of five years.
4. The $12,000 received in November 2008 for work to be done has now been earned.
5. The note dated July 1, 2008, is payable in 2011 and bears interest at 8 percent per year. Interest is payable annually on July 1.
6. Services provided to other customers but not billed at December 31, 2008, total $3,500.
7. Salaries of $2,500 are unpaid at December 31, 2008.

Instructions
Prepare the adjusting entries for the year ending December 31, 2008. (Hint: do not use the Cash account in the solution.)

Solution to Demonstration Problem

General Journal			J1
Date	**Account Titles and Explanation**	**Debit**	**Credit**
2008			
Dec. 31	Supplies Expense	5,500	
	Supplies		5,500
	$8,500 − $3,000		
31	Insurance Expense	7,000	
	Prepaid Insurance		7,000
	$12,000 x 7/12		
31	Amortization Expense	8,000	
	Accumulated Amortization—Equipment		8,000
	$40,000 ÷ 5		
31	Unearned Revenue	12,000	
	Service Revenue		12,000
31	Interest Expense	2,000	
	Interest Payable		2,000
	$50,000 x 8% x 6/12		
31	Accounts Receivable	3,500	
	Service Revenue		3,500
31	Salaries Expense	2,500	
	Salaries Payable		2,500

Review Questions and Exercises
Multiple Choice

Circle the letter that best answers each of the following statements.

1. (SO 1) The time period assumption assumes that:
    a. revenue should be recognized in the accounting period in which it is earned.
    b. the economic life of a business can be divided into artificial time periods.
    c. expenses should be matched with revenues.
    d. the fiscal year should correspond with the calendar year.

2. (SO 1) The revenue recognition principle states that:
    a. revenue should be recognized in the accounting period in which it is earned.
    b. a business can recognize revenue when it is received, depending on the type of business it operates.
    c. expenses should be matched with revenues.
    d. the fiscal year should correspond with the calendar year.

3. (SO 1) The matching principle dictates that:
    a. each debit has to be matched with an equal credit.
    b. revenue should be recognized in the accounting period in which it is earned.
    c. expenses should be matched with revenues.
    d. the fiscal year should match the calendar year.

4. (SO 1) Which of the following statements concerning the accrual basis of accounting is incorrect?
    a. The accrual basis of accounting follows the revenue recognition principle.
    b. The accrual basis of accounting is the method required by generally accepted accounting principles.
    c. The accrual basis of accounting recognizes expenses when they are incurred for the purpose of earning revenues.
    d. The accrual basis of accounting follows the matching principle.

5. (SO 1) Under the accrual basis of accounting:
    a. revenue is recognized when it is received in cash.
    b. transactions that change a company's financial statements are recorded in the period in which the event occurs.
    c. it is not necessary to accumulate expenses incurred.
    d. adjusting entries are journalized throughout the year.

6. (SO 2) For prepaid expense adjusting entries:
    a. an expense–liability account relationship exists.
    b. expenses are overstated and assets are understated prior to adjustment.
    c. the adjusting entry results in a debit to an expense account and a credit to an asset account.
    d. none of the above.

7. (SO 2) The beginning balance of Supplies for Lu Company was $900. During the year additional supplies were purchased for $450. At the end of the year an inventory count indicates that $700 of supplies are on hand. The adjusting entry at December 31 is:

   a. Supplies   650
          Supplies Expense   650
   b. Supplies   450
          Supplies Expense   450
   c. Supplies Expense   250
          Supplies   250
   d. Supplies Expense   650
          Supplies   650

8. (SO 2) Damian Cruise Lines purchased a one-year insurance policy for its ships on April 1, 2008, for $20,000. Assuming that April 1 is the effective date of the policy, the adjusting entry on December 31, 2008, is:

   a. Prepaid Insurance   15,000
          Insurance Expense   15,000
   b. Insurance Expense   15,000
          Prepaid Insurance   15,000
   c. Insurance Expense   20,000
          Prepaid Insurance   20,000
   d. Insurance Expense   5,000
          Prepaid Insurance   5,000

9. (SO 2) For unearned revenue adjusting entries, which of the following statements is incorrect?

   a. A liability–revenue account relationship exists.
   b. Prior to adjustment, revenues are overstated and liabilities are understated.
   c. The adjusting entry results in a debit to a liability account and a credit to a revenue account.
   d. If the adjustment is not made, revenues will be understated.

10. (SO 2) On May 1, 2008, Marcel Advertising Company received $3,000 from Kathy Siska for advertising services to be completed by April 30, 2009. At December 31, 2008, $2,000 of the revenue has been earned. The adjusting entry on December 31, 2008, by Marcel will include a:

    a. $1,000 credit to Unearned Advertising Revenue.
    b. $1,000 debit to Advertising Revenue.
    c. $2,000 credit to Unearned Advertising Revenue.
    d. $2,000 debit to Unearned Advertising Revenue.

11. (SO 2) The account Unearned Revenue is a(n):

    a. revenue account.
    b. contra revenue account.
    c. liability account.
    d. asset account.

12. (SO 2) Cost less accumulated amortization is often called:

    a. net book value.

    b. market value.

    c. original value.

    d. none of the above.

13. (SO 3) For accrued revenue adjusting entries:

    a. an asset–revenue account relationship exists.

    b. assets and revenues are both overstated prior to adjustment.

    c. the adjusting entry results in a debit to a revenue account and a credit to an asset account.

    d. none of the above.

14. (SO 3) On June 30, Zhang Marketing Services is preparing its financial statements. Fees in the amount of $600 were earned in June but have not been billed to clients or recorded by June 30. The adjusting entry at June 30 is:

    a. Unearned Marketing Revenue   600

        Marketing Revenue   600

    b. Accounts Receivable   600

        Marketing Revenue   600

    c. Marketing Revenue   600

        Accounts Receivable   600

    d. Marketing Revenue   600

        Unearned Marketing Revenue   600

15. (SO 3) For accrued expense adjusting entries, which of the following statements is incorrect?

    a. A liability–expense account relationship exists.

    b. Prior to adjustment, both expenses and liabilities are understated.

    c. If the adjusting entry is not made, expenses will be overstated on the income statement.

    d. The adjusting entry results in a debit to an expense account and a credit to a liability account.

16. (SO 3) Gardner Company purchased a truck from Kutner Co. by issuing a six-month, 9 percent note payable for $30,000 on November 1. On December 31, Gardner's accrued expense adjusting entry is:

    a. No entry is required.

    b. Interest Expense   3,000

        Interest Payable   3,000

    c. Interest Expense   6,000

        Interest Payable   6,000

    d. Interest Expense   450

        Interest Payable   450

17. (SO 3) Cathy Cline, an employee of Wheeler Company, will not be paid until April 2. Based on services performed from March 15 to March 30 her salary was $800. The adjusting entry for Wheeler Company on March 31 is:

  a. Salaries Expense   800
          Salaries Payable   800
  b. No entry is required.
  c. Salaries Expense   800
          Cash   800
  d. Salaries Payable   800
          Cash   800

18. (SO 4) The adjusted trial balance can be used for the preparation of:

  a. the income statement.
  b. the balance sheet.
  c. the statement of owner's equity.
  d. all of the above.

19. (SO 4) All of the following statements about the preparation of financial statements are correct except:

  a. the balance sheet is prepared from the asset and liability accounts and the ending owner's capital balance that is reported on the statement of owner's equity.
  b. the balance sheet is prepared first, then the income statement, then the statement of owner's equity.
  c. the statement of owner's equity is prepared from the owner's capital and drawings accounts and from net income (or net loss) shown on the income statement.
  d. the income statement is prepared from the revenue and expense accounts.

20. (SO 4) Financial statements are prepared directly from the:

  a. general journal.
  b. chart of accounts.
  c. trial balance.
  d. adjusted trial balance.

21. (SO 4) All of the following statements are correct about the adjusted trial balance except:

  a. it proves the equality of the total debits and credits.
  b. it makes it easier to prepare the financial statements.
  c. the totals of the adjusted trial balance columns must be equal to the totals of the balance sheet since all the statements prepared from the adjusted trial balance flow into the balance sheet.
  d. it contains all the necessary data needed up to the adjustment date.

*22.(SO 5) Pillai Co. purchased $8,000 worth of supplies during the fiscal year. All purchases were recorded in the Supplies Expense account. At year end, October 31, a count showed that $6,500 worth of supplies have been used up. The adjusting entry is:

a. Supplies Expense   1,500
        Supplies   1,500
b. Supplies   1,500
        Supplies Expense   1,500
c. Supplies Expense   6,500
        Supplies   6,500
d. Supplies   6,500
        Supplies Expense   6,500

*23.(SO 5) The Service Revenue account of Acquinas Architects showed a balance of $70,000 at the end of the period. When the account was analyzed, services in the amount of $5,000 had not yet been completed. The adjusting entry at the end of the period is:

a. Service Revenue   65,000
        Unearned Revenue   65,000
b. Unearned Revenue   65,000
        Service Revenue   65,000
c. Service Revenue   5,000
        Unearned Revenue   5,000
d. Unearned Revenue   5,000
        Service Revenue   5,000

*24.(SO 5) The Accounting Revenue account of Jamey Accounting Associates showed a balance of $70,000 at the end of the period. When the client accounts were analyzed, it was determined that services in the amount of $45,000 had been completed. The adjusting entry at the end of the period is:

a. Accounting Revenue   45,000
        Unearned Revenue   45,000
b. Unearned Revenue   45,000
        Accounting Revenue   45,000
c. Accounting Revenue   25,000
        Unearned Revenue   25,000
d. Unearned Revenue   25,000
        Accounting Revenue   25,000

Matching

Match each term with its definition by writing the appropriate letter in the space provided.

Terms

_____ 1. Amortization

_____ 2. Time period assumption

_____ 3. Matching principle

_____ 4. Revenue recognition

_____ 5. Fiscal years

_____ 6. Contra asset account

_____ 7. Adjusted trial balance

_____ 8. Unearned revenues

_____ 9. Adjusting entries

_____ 10. Accrued revenues

_____ 11. Prepaid expenses

_____ 12. Cash basis of accounting

_____ 13. Accrued expenses

_____ 14. Accrual basis of accounting

Definitions

a. An account that is offset against an asset account on the balance sheet.

b. Costs paid in cash and recorded in an asset account before they are used or consumed.

c. Revenues earned but not yet received or recorded at the statement date.

d. Accounting periods that are one year in length.

e. The principle that efforts (expenses) should be matched with accomplishments (revenues).

f. An accounting basis in which events that change a company's financial statements are recorded in the period in which the event occurs.

g. Expenses incurred but not yet paid or recorded at the statement date.

h. A list of accounts and their balances after all adjustments have been made.

i. The assumption that the economic life of a business can be divided into artificial time periods.

j. Revenue is recorded only when cash is received, and an expense is recorded only when cash is paid.

k. The process of allocating the cost of a long-lived asset to expense over its useful life in a rational and systematic manner.

l. Cash received and recorded as an accounting liability before it is earned.

m. Entries made at the end of the accounting period to ensure that the revenue recognition and matching principles are followed.

n. The principle that revenue be recognized in the accounting period in which it is earned.

Exercises

E3-1   (SO 2 & 3) McDaniels Painting Company is at the end of its fiscal year, December 31, 2008, and needs to record its adjusting entries. Adjustment data are as follows:

a. Four months ago, Judy Bernstein made an $8,000 prepayment for the painting of her house. McDaniels recorded the original entry as unearned revenue. At December 31, one-fourth of the house remains to be painted.

b. McDaniels purchased a truck from Donnelly Vehicles on January 1, 2005, at a cost of $20,000. The truck is expected to have a useful life of five years.

c. An employee, Pam Travis, earned wages of $500 for the last week in December. She will not be paid until January 5.

d. McDaniels purchased a $6,000, one-year insurance policy from Heinsen Insurance four months ago. The effective date of the policy was September 1, 2008.

e. McDaniels began painting Peggy Thompson's clubhouse in November at a price of $32,000. McDaniels determines that $20,000 of the revenue has been earned at December 31. Thompson has not made any payment to McDaniels, and McDaniels has not billed Thompson for services performed.

f. McDaniels has a $25,000, 6 percent note payable. Interest is paid on the first of each month for the previous month.

Instructions
Prepare the adjusting entries at December 31, 2008.

Date	Account Titles and Explanation	Debit	Credit
2008			
a.			
b.			
c.			
d.			
e.			
f.			

General Journal   JI

E3-2   (SO 2) The Webster Company bought office equipment on July 1, 2008, at a cost of $54,000, paying $10,000 cash and signing a note payable for the remainder. The equipment is expected to have a useful life of nine years.

Instructions
(a) Record the purchase of the office equipment on July 1.

_____

_____

(b) Calculate the annual amortization expense.

_____

_____

(c) Prepare the adjusting journal entry to record the amortization at December 31, 2008.

_____

_____

(d) Show the statement presentation at December 31, 2008, the company's year end.

_____

_____

_____

_____

_____

_____

E3-3   (SO 2)

(a) Explain the asset–expense relationship between prepaid insurance and the related adjusting entry when the asset is used up.

_____

_____

(b) Explain the asset–expense relationship between a long-lived asset (e.g., buildings) and the related adjusting entry as the asset is used up.

_____

_____

(c) What is the difference in the impact of these two adjusting entries on statement presentation?

_____

_____

E3-4   (SO 4) The adjusted trial balance of Susan Marowally Company at November 30, 2008, is as follows:

SUSAN MAROWALLY COMPANY
Adjusted Trial Balance
November 30, 2008

	Debit	Credit
Cash	$ 7,250	
Accounts Receivable	17,000	
Supplies	500	
Prepaid Insurance	2,500	
Land	12,000	
Equipment	40,000	
Accumulated Amortization—Equipment		$16,000
Notes Payable		7,500
Accounts Payable		5,950
Interest Payable		350
Unearned Revenue		7,500
Salaries Payable		5,000
S. Marowally, Capital		38,000
Service Revenue		19,700
Salaries Expense	11,500	
Supplies Expense	400	
Rent Expense	2,000	
Insurance Expense	2,500	
Amortization Expense	4,000	
Interest Expense	350	
	$100,000	$100,000

Instructions

(a) Prepare an income statement and a statement of owner's equity for the year ended November 30, 2008. The owner made no additional investments during the year.

(a)

SUSAN MAROWALLY COMPANY
Income Statement
Year Ended November 30, 2008

SUSAN MAROWALLY COMPANY
Statement of Owner's Equity
Year Ended November 30, 2008

(b) Prepare a balance sheet at November 30, 2008.

SUSAN MAROWALLY
Balance Sheet
November 30, 2005

*E3-5   (SO 5) Ivanhoe prepares annual adjusting entries and financial statements at December 31. During the year ended December 31, 2008, Ivanhoe had the following transactions:

June 1   A one-year insurance policy was purchased, with coverage to take effect on June 1, 2008, for $3,600.

Dec. 1   A customer paid $5,000 for services to be performed before March 31, 2009. At December 31, Ivanhoe had performed $1,500 of the services.

Instructions

(a) Assume that Ivanhoe Company uses the alternative treatment to record prepayments. That is, Ivanhoe records all prepaid costs as expenses and all revenue collected in advance as revenues.
  1. Record the June 1 and December 1 transactions.
  2. Prepare any necessary adjusting entries Ivanhoe would make at December 31, 2008, to satisfy the matching and revenue recognition principles.

(b) Assume instead that Ivanhoe Company records all prepaid costs as assets and all revenue collected in advance as liabilities.
  1. Record the June 1 and December 1 transactions.
  2. Prepare any necessary adjusting entries Ivanhoe would make at December 31, 2008, to satisfy the matching and revenue recognition principles.

	General Journal		J1
Date	**Account Titles and Explanation**	**Debit**	**Credit**
2008			

Solutions to Review Questions and Exercises

Multiple Choice

1. (b) Choice (a) is the revenue recognition principle. Choice (c) is the matching principle. Answer (d) pertains to the time periods, but the fiscal year does not have to correspond to the calendar year.

2. (a) Choice (b) is the cash method of recognizing revenue when it is received. Choice (c) is a cash method statement. Answer (d) is an incorrect statement, because the fiscal year does not necessarily have to be the calendar year.

3. (c) Choice (a) is the basis of the balance sheet equation. Choice (b) is the revenue recognition principle. Choice (d) is not necessarily so, because the fiscal year is not always a calendar year.

4. (c) The accrual basis of accounting recognizes expenses when they are incurred for the purpose of earning revenue. Choices (a), (b), and (d) are all correct statements concerning the accrual basis of accounting.

5. (b) Choices (a), (c), and (d) are all untrue. Choice (b) is correct, because under the accrual basis of accounting transactions are recognized in the period in which the events occur, not when cash is paid or received.

6. (c) Answer (a) is incorrect because an asset–expense account relationship exists. Answer (b) is incorrect because assets are overstated and expenses are understated prior to adjustment.

7. (d) The total cost of supplies is $1,350 ($900 + $450). Since the ending inventory is $700, the supplies expense for the period is $650 ($1,350 – $700).

8. (b) Because the effective date of the policy is April 1, only 3/4 of one year is expensed ($20,000 x 9/12 = $15,000). Insurance Expense is debited and Prepaid Insurance is credited because the $20,000 payment was debited to Prepaid Insurance.

9. (b) Prior to adjustment, liabilities are overstated and revenues are understated. The other choices are correct.

10. (d) The account balances should be Unearned Advertising Revenue, $1,000 credit, and Advertising Revenue, $2,000 credit. Thus, the adjusting entry is:

    Unearned Advertising Revenue   2,000
         Advertising Revenue   2,000

11. (c) Unearned Revenue is the receipt of cash or an asset before the service has been performed. The obligation to perform this service is indicated in the records by crediting a liability account.

12.   (a)   The market value (b) is the current exchange value of the asset. The original value (c) would refer to the cost.

13.   (a)   Answer (b) is incorrect because both assets and revenues are understated prior to adjustment. Answer (c) is incorrect because an asset account is debited and a revenue account is credited.

14.   (b)   The amount owed by the client is a receivable that is debited to an asset account. The services concerning this receivable have been performed and thus earned; therefore, a revenue account is credited.

15.   (c)   In an accrued expense adjusting entry, expenses are understated prior to adjustment as in choice (b). Therefore, if the adjusting entry is not made, expenses will be understated.

16.   (d)   The accrued interest is $450 ($30,000 x 9% x 2/12).

17.   (a)   The accrued expense is recognized by debiting Salaries Expense and crediting Salaries Payable.

18.   (d)   All of the statements (a), (b), and (c) can be prepared from the adjusted trial balance.

19.   (b)   Choices (a), (c), and (d) are all correct. Choice (b) is incorrect because the income statement is prepared first, then the statement of owner's equity, and then the balance sheet.

20.   (d)   The adjusted trial balance is prepared after all adjusting entries have been posted. Accordingly, the financial statements can be prepared directly from it.

21.   (c)   Choices (a), (b), and (d) are all correct. The sum of the balances in the adjusted trial balance will not equal the balance sheet totals. Balances in the adjusted trial balance are presented differently in the statements from the way in which they are used in the adjusted trial balance.

*22.   (b)   When the alternative treatment of recording supplies is used and the purchases are in the Supplies Expense account, the adjustment must credit the expense account and debit the asset account.

*23.   (c)   Using the alternative treatment where cash receipts are credited to the revenue account, on adjustment the revenue account is reduced with a debit to reflect the amount not yet earned.

*24.   (c)   The revenue account (normal credit balance) should show a balance of $45,000. Therefore, it must be debited in the amount of $25,000 to decrease the account. The credit would be made to unearned revenue, a liability account.

Matching

1.	k	5.	d	9.	m	13.	g
2.	i	6.	a	10.	c	14.	f
3.	e	7.	h	11.	b		
4.	n	8.	l	12.	j		

Exercises

E3-1

General Journal			JI

Date	Account Titles and Explanation	Debit	Credit
	Adjusting Entries		
a.	Unearned Painting Revenue	6,000	
	Painting Revenue		6,000
	To record revenue earned on completion of 75% of project.		
b.	Amortization Expense	4,000	
	Accumulated Amortization—Truck		4,000
	To record annual amortization: $20,000 ÷ 5.		
c.	Wages Expense	500	
	Wages Payable		500
	To record accrued wages.		
d.	Insurance Expense	2,000	
	Prepaid Insurance		2,000
	To record insurance expired: $6,000 x 4/12.		
e.	Accounts Receivable	20,000	
	Painting Revenue		20,000
	To accrue revenue earned.		
f.	Interest Expense	125	
	Interest Payable		125
	To accrue interest expense: $25,000 x 6% x1/12.		

E3-2

(a) Jul. 1   Office Equipment   54,000
                    Cash   10,000
                    Note Payable   44,000
              To record purchase of office equipment

(b) Cost ÷ Useful life   =   Amortization expense
        $54,000 ÷ 9   = $6,000

(c) 2008
      Dec. 31   Amortization Expense   3,000
                      Accumulated Amortization
                      —Office Equipment   3,000
              To record amortization July 1–Dec. 31: $6,000 x 6/12

(d) Office Equipment $54,000
     Less: Accumulated Amortization—Office equipment   3,000*
     Net book value $51,000
     * $6,000 x 1/2 years = $3,000

E3-3

(a) Prepaid insurance is originally recorded as an asset. As the insurance is used up, the company no longer has an asset—instead it has an expense. The asset must then be reduced, otherwise assets will be overstated and expenses understated. When the insurance is used up, Insurance Expense is debited and Prepaid Insurance is credited.

(b) Long-lived assets are originally recorded as assets and are, in fact, a long-term payment for services. As the long-lived asset is used up, it is necessary to recognize the cost that has been used up (the expense) during the period, and report the unused cost (the asset) at the end of the period. The account Amortization Expense is debited and the account Accumulated Amortization is credited. The using up of the asset over its useful life is accumulated in the Accumulated Amortization account, which is a contra account to the asset.

(c) Both adjusting entries will result in an expense being presented on the income statement. The difference is on the balance sheet. There is no special presentation for the prepaid insurance—the amount shown on the balance sheet is equal to the amount of unexpired insurance. However, for long-lived assets, the original asset account is not reduced as the asset is used up because it is useful to present information about the original cost of the long-lived assets on the balance sheet. Instead, the amount of the long-lived asset that has been used up to the statement date is recorded in an Accumulated Amortization account. The original cost of the asset and the accumulated amortization are both presented on the balance sheet. The accumulated amortization is subtracted from the original cost to show the net book value of the long-lived asset.

E3-4

(a)

SUSAN MAROWALLY
Income Statement
Year Ended November 30, 2008

Revenues		
Service Revenue		$19,700
Expenses		
Salaries expense	$11,500	
Supplies expense	400	
Rent expense	2,000	
Insurance expense	2,500	
Amortization expense	4,000	
Interest expense	350	
Total expenses		20,750
Net loss		$ 1,050

SUSAN MAROWALLY
Statement of Owner's Equity
Year Ended November 30, 2008

S. Marowally, Capital, December 1, 2007	$38,000
Less: Net loss	1,050
S. Marowally, Capital, November 30, 2008	$36,950

(b)

SUSAN MAROWALLY
Balance Sheet
November 30, 2008

Assets

Cash		$ 7,250
Accounts receivable		17,000
Supplies		500
Prepaid insurance		2,500
Land		12,000
Equipment	$40,000	
Less: Accumulated amortization—Equipment	16,000	24,000
Total assets		$63,250

Liabilities and Owner's Equity

Liabilities		
Notes payable		$ 7,500
Accounts payable		5,950
Interest payable		350
Unearned revenue		7,500
Salaries payable		5,000
Total liabilities		26,300
Owner's Equity		
S. Marowally, Capital		36,950
Total liabilities and owner's equity		$ 63,250

---

*E3-5

General Journal			JI
Date	**Account Titles and Explanation**	**Debit**	**Credit**
2008			
(a)			
1.	**Transactions**		
Jun. 1	Insurance Expense	3,600	
	Cash		3,600
	To record the purchase of a one-year insurance policy.		
Dec. 1	Cash	5,000	
	Service Revenue		5,000
	To record cash collected from customer.		

	General Journal		J1
Date	**Account Titles and Explanation**	**Debit**	**Credit**
2008			
2.	**Adjusting Entries**		
Dec. 31	Prepaid Insurance	1,500	
	Insurance Expense		1,500
	To record unexpired insurance: $3,600 × 5/12.		
31	Service Revenue	3,500	
	Unearned Service Revenue		3,500
	To record unearned service revenue: $5,000 − $1,500.		
(b)			
1.	**Transactions**		
Jun. 1	Prepaid Insurance	3,600	
	Cash		3,600
	To record the purchase of a one-year insurance policy		
Dec. 1	Cash	5,000	
	Unearned Service Revenue		5,000
	To record cash collected from customer		
2.	**Adjusting Entries**		
Dec. 31	Insurance Expense	2,100	
	Prepaid Insurance		2,100
	To record expired insurance: $3,600 × 7/12		
31	Unearned Service Revenue	1,500	
	Service Revenue		1,500
	To record earned service revenue		

chapter 4

Completion of the Accounting Cycle

study objectives >>

After studying this chapter, you should be able to:
1. Prepare closing entries and a post-closing trial balance.
2. List the steps in the accounting cycle.
3. Prepare correcting entries.
4. Prepare a classified balance sheet.
5. Illustrate measures used to evaluate liquidity.
6. Prepare a work sheet (Appendix 4A).
7. Prepare reversing entries (Appendix 4B).

Preview of Chapter 4

In Chapter 3 we prepared the financial statements directly from the adjusted trial balance. In this chapter we will explain the remaining steps in the accounting cycle—especially the closing process. We will also consider correcting entries and classified balance sheets. The chapter is organized as follows:

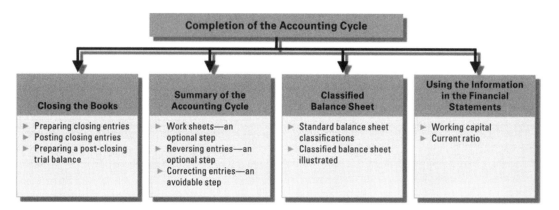

Closing the Books

Closing the books occurs at the end of an accounting period when the accounts are made ready for the next accounting period. To do this, it is necessary to distinguish between temporary and permanent accounts. Temporary accounts only collect data for a single period. Permanent accounts have their balances carried forward into the next accounting period.

Temporary Accounts	Permanent Accounts
Accounts closed	**Accounts not closed**
Revenue accounts	Asset accounts
Expense accounts	Liability accounts
Owner's drawings account	Owner's capital account

Preparing Closing Entries

study objective 1

Prepare closing entries and a post-closing trial balance.

Closing entries are used to transfer the temporary accounts (revenue, expenses, and owner's drawings) to owner's capital. The accounts that pertain to net income (or net loss) and the owner's drawings are recorded in the ledger. Closing entries result in a zero balance in each temporary account. The temporary accounts are now ready to collect data in the next accounting period.

Journalizing and posting closing entries are required steps in the accounting cycle. This process is performed after financial statements have been prepared and normally occurs at the end of a company's annual accounting period.

In computerized accounting systems, the closing process occurs automatically when it is time to start a new accounting period. In manual accounting systems, the revenue and expense accounts are closed to another temporary account, Income Summary. The Income Summary account is then checked to make sure it is equal to the net income or net loss for the period.

Once that is done, the net income or the net loss can then be transferred from the Income Summary account to owner's capital.

To close the books, follow these four steps:
1. **Close revenue accounts**: Debit each individual revenue account for its balance, and credit Income Summary for total revenues.
2. **Close expense accounts**: Debit Income Summary for total expenses, and credit each individual expense account for its balance.
3. **Close Income Summary**: Debit Income Summary for its balance (or credit if a net loss), and credit (or debit) Owner's Capital.
4. **Close Drawings**: Debit Owner's Capital and credit Owner's Drawings for the balance in the drawings account.

TIP

To ensure that closing entries have been correctly prepared, the balance of the Income Summary account, after steps 1 and 2 above, must be equal to the net income (or net loss). After the four closing entries have been posted to the ledger, the balance in Owner's Capital must agree with the amount shown as an ending balance on the statement of owner's equity and the balance sheet.

Preparing a Post-Closing Trial Balance

After all closing entries have been journalized and posted, a post-closing trial balance is prepared. The purpose of this trial balance is to prove the equality of the permanent account balances that are carried forward into the next accounting period.

The post-closing trial balance lists only permanent accounts—asset accounts, liability accounts, and owner's capital. It provides evidence that the journalizing and posting of closing entries has been completed properly.

TIP

Do not confuse a post-closing trial balance and a balance sheet. A trial balance is a listing of all accounts in the ledger to prove the mathematical equality of debits and credits—it is not a financial statement. A balance sheet is the financial statement that lists assets, liabilities, and owner's equity.

Summary of the Accounting Cycle

The steps in the accounting cycle are done in sequence and are repeated in each accounting period. They are as follows:

study objective 2

List the steps in the accounting cycle.

1. Analyze business transactions.
2. Journalize the transactions.
3. Post to ledger accounts.
4. Prepare a trial balance.
5. Journalize and post adjusting entries—prepayments/accruals.
6. Prepare an adjusted trial balance.
7. Prepare financial statements—income statement, statement of owner's equity, balance sheet.
8. Journalize and post closing entries.
9. Prepare a post-closing trial balance.

After these nine steps you have completed an entire accounting cycle!

There are also two optional steps in the accounting cycle: (1) a work sheet may be used in the adjustment process when preparing the financial statements, and (2) reversing entries may be used at the beginning of the new accounting period.

Work Sheets—An Optional Step

A work sheet is a multiple-column form that accountants may use to prepare adjusting entries and the financial statements. Work sheets can be prepared manually. However, most work sheets are prepared using accounting software or a spreadsheet program.

A work sheet is not a permanent accounting record; a work sheet is a tool that makes it easier to prepare adjusting entries and financial statements. Though optional, work sheets are useful because they help accountants avoid errors when working with a lot of information that involves many accounts and adjustments.

The obvious benefit of using a spreadsheet is that data can be changed, as required, and calculations are automatically updated. Statements for interim periods can also be easily prepared.

Reversing Entries—An Optional Step

In some cases, certain adjusting entries are reversed at the beginning of the new accounting period. The reversing entry is the exact opposite of the adjusting entry made in the previous period. This is an optional bookkeeping procedure, not a required step in the accounting cycle.

Correcting Entries—An Avoidable Step

study objective 3

Prepare correcting entries.

Correcting entries are entries to correct errors that have occurred during the recording process. They should not be confused with adjusting entries, which are a necessary part of the accounting cycle. Correcting entries are journalized and posted when financial statements are prepared, usually at the end of an accounting period.

Errors should be corrected as soon as they are discovered by journalizing and posting correcting entries. If there are no errors in the accounting records, no correcting entries are needed. Both correcting entries and adjusting entries must be journalized and posted before closing entries are posted at the end of the accounting period.

The following example will help illustrate different approaches to preparing a correcting entry.

On June 15, Archer Company invoices a customer for $3,500 of services performed. On that date the entry is correctly recorded in Archer's books as:

Accounts Receivable	3,500	
Service Revenue		3,500
To record services rendered on account		

On July 14, when payment is received, Archer's accounting clerk incorrectly records the following entry:

Cash	3,500	
Service Revenue		3,500
To record collection of services provided on account		

There are two equally acceptable approaches to preparing the correcting entry:

1. Include only the differences between the incorrect accounts and correct accounts:

Service Revenue	3,500	
Accounts receivable		3,500
To correct error in recording July 14 cash receipt		

2. Reverse the incorrect entry and then record the correct entry:

Service Revenue	3,500	
Cash		3,500
To reverse incorrect posting of July 14 cash receipt		
Cash	3,500	
Accounts Receivable		3,500
To correctly post July 14 cash receipt		

Classified Balance Sheet

Financial statements become more useful in decision making when the elements are classified into significant subgroups. A classified balance sheet is not as simple as the balance sheet outlined in previous chapters. For a classified balance sheet, we classify assets, liabilities, and owner's equity on the balance sheet, and revenues and expenses on the income statement.

study objective 4

Prepare a classified balance sheet.

Standard Balance Sheet Classifications

Assets	Liabilities and Owner's Equity
Current assets	Current liabilities
Long-term investments	Long-term liabilities
Property, plant, and equipment	Owner's equity
Intangible assets	

Current Assets

Current assets are cash and other resources that will be realized (consumed) in the business within one year of the balance sheet date. Current assets are listed in the order of their liquidity; that is, the order in which they are expected to be converted into cash. Typically, a current asset listing would include cash and cash equivalents, short-term investments, accounts receivable, recoverable items, and prepaid expenses. A company's current assets are important in assessing its short-term debt-paying ability.

Long-Term Investments

Long-term investments are investments in other companies. These debts or shares are expected to be held for many years. Examples of long-term investments are shares bought in another company, bonds of other corporations, loans made to other companies or persons, and real estate intended for future use. All of these are not intended to be quickly converted to cash. Typically, the long-term investment section would include shares, bonds, mortgage and other loans (receivable), and real estate.

Property, Plant, and Equipment

Property, plant, and equipment (PP&E) are long-lived, tangible resources used in the operation of the business and are not intended for sale. Also known as capital or fixed assets, they include land, buildings, equipment, and furniture.

PP&E are listed on the balance sheet in order of permanency. Land is usually listed first because it has an indefinite life, followed by buildings, furniture, and equipment. The cost of these assets—including their contra asset account, Accumulated Amortization—are reported on the financial statements as net book value (cost minus accumulated amortization). Typically, the property, plant, and equipment section would include the following:

> Land
> Building
> Less: Accumulated amortization—building
> Furniture
> Less: Accumulated amortization—furniture
> Equipment
> Less: Accumulated amortization—equipment

TIP

When preparing a classified balance sheet, remember that the accumulated amortization account is a contra asset account. Though it has a normal credit balance, it is an asset and must be listed with the asset to which it relates.

Refer to the demonstration problem at the end of Chapter 4 in the text about Paquet Answering Service. Note the use of three columns in the presentation of property, plant, and equipment. Land is listed by itself in the middle column because it does not have a contra account. Building and Equipment are listed in the first column and followed by their respective contra accounts. Note how the net book value of the building and the equipment are carried to the middle column and added to land to become part of the total in the third column.

Intangible Assets

Intangible assets are long-lived assets that do not have any physical substance. They include such things as goodwill, patents, copyrights, trademarks, trade names, and licences. Intangibles with estimated useful lives are amortized; those with indefinite lives are not amortized.

Current Liabilities

Current liabilities are obligations that are expected to be paid from current assets or paid by creating other current liabilities within one year. Current liabilities are often listed in the order they come due. Current liabilities would include accounts payable, accrued liabilities, and in some cases the principal payments on long-term obligations due within one year.

Long-Term Liabilities

Long-term liabilities are obligations expected to be paid after one year. Typical examples of long-term liabilities include bonds payable, mortgages payable, and long-term notes payable. Some companies may show the details of the debt in the notes that accompany the financial statements.

Equity

The content of the owner's equity section varies with the form of business organization. In a proprietorship, there is a single owner's equity account. In a partnership, there is a separate capital account for each partner under the heading "Partners' equity." For a corporation, owner's equity is called shareholders' equity, and it consists of two sections: share capital (sometimes called capital stock) and retained earnings.

Classified Balance Sheet Presentation

A balance sheet is usually presented in report form, with the assets shown above the liabilities and owner's equity (see Illustration 4-13 in the text). Note the use of headings for each category of assets and liabilities. Note also how each classification requires a total.

The balance sheet may also be presented in account form, with the assets section placed on the left and the liabilities and owner's equity sections on the right.

Using the Information in the Financial Statements

Investors use information in the financial statements to decide if they should invest in a business. Creditors use the information to decide if they should grant credit to a business. Ratio analysis is the tool used to express relationships between specific items in the financial statements.

study objective 5

Illustrate measures used to evaluate liquidity.

Liquidity is the company's ability to pay its obligations as they become due and to meet unexpected needs for cash. Two measurements of liquidity are introduced in this chapter: working capital and the current ratio.

Working capital is an important measure of a company's liquidity. It is determined by subtracting total current liabilities from total current assets. Working capital represents the company's ability to pay obligations that become due within the next year.

Refer to Illustration 4-13 to calculate Pioneer Advertising Agency's working capital:

Current Assets	–	Current Liabilities	=	Working Capital
$16,950	–	$6,325	=	$10,625

The current ratio measures the relationship of current assets to current liabilities. It is calculated by dividing total current assets by total current liabilities.

Pioneer's current ratio:

Current Assets	÷	Current Liabilities	=	Current Ratio
$16,950	÷	$6,325	=	2.68:1

This ratio indicates that Pioneer has $2.68 in current assets to pay every $1.00 in current liabilities.

Together with the ratios mentioned above, additional factors must be considered when using ratio analysis: (1) general economic and industry conditions, (2) specific financial information about the company over time, and (3) ratios of other companies in the same or related industries.

Appendix 4A

Work Sheets

study objective 6

Prepare a work sheet (Appendix 4A).

Refer to Illustration 4A-1 in the text to follow the steps for preparing a work sheet.

Step 1   Prepare a trial balance on the work sheet.

Step 2   Enter the adjustments in the adjustment columns.

Step 3   Enter the adjusted balances in the adjusted trial balance columns. Financial statements can only be prepared from the adjusted trial balance.

Step 4   Enter the adjusted trial balance amounts in the income statement or balance sheet columns of the work sheet. Enter adjusted balances for revenue and expense amounts in the income statement columns. Enter adjusted balances for asset, liability, and owner's equity amounts in the balance sheet columns.

Step 5   Total the statement columns and calculate net income (or net loss) to complete the work sheet. The net income or loss for the period is found by calculating the difference between the totals of the two income statement columns. Net income results if total credits are more than total debits; a net loss results when total debits are more than total credits. Using an electronic spreadsheet simplifies this step and allows for ease of calculating net income (or net loss).

Note that the differences between the columns of the income statement and the balance sheet columns must be the same because this difference is the net income (or net loss).

Preparing Financial Statements from a Work Sheet

When a work sheet is complete, all the data required to prepare the financial statements is available. Accountants can prepare the statements before adjusting entries have been journalized and posted. They can even produce a post-closing trial balance.

The income statement is prepared from the income statement columns. The balance sheet and statement of owner's equity are prepared from the balance sheet columns. However, remember that the work sheet is not a substitute for formal financial statements. It is basically an accountant's working tool and is not distributed to management or other parties.

Appendix 4B

Reversing Entries

study objective 7

Prepare reversing entries (Appendix 4B).

After financial statements have been prepared and the books are closed, some of the adjusting entries may be reversed before the regular transactions for the next period are recorded. A reversing entry is the exact opposite of an adjusting entry made in the previous period. The preparation of reversing entries is an optional bookkeeping procedure that is not a required step in the accounting cycle.

Made at the beginning of the next accounting period to simplify the recording of subsequent transactions related to the adjusting entries, reversing entries are most often used with two types of adjusting entries: accrued revenues and accrued expenses.

The following example will illustrate the difference in recording a transaction for accrued expense when reversing entries are made and when reversing entries are not made.

On December 31, 2007, a company has accrued salary expense of $900, representing salaries earned but unpaid for the last day of December. The company normally pays salaries on Friday. On Friday, January 4, 2008, total weekly wages paid (December 31 plus four days worked in 2008) are $4,500. The company will record the following journal entries in December and January:

No reversing entries are made:

Dec. 31, 2007	Salary Expense	900	
	Salaries Payable		900
	To record accrued salaries		

Dec. 31, 2007	Income Summary	900	
	Salaries Expense		900
	To close Salaries Expense to Income Summary		

Jan. 4, 2008	Salary Expense	3,600	
	Salaries Payable	900	
	Cash		4,500
	To record payment of salaries		

Reversing entries are made:

Dec. 31, 2007	Salary Expense	900	
	Salaries Payable		900
	To record accrued salaries		

Dec. 31, 2007	Income Summary	900	
	Salaries Expense		900
	To close Salaries Expense to Income Summary		

Jan. 1, 2008	Salaries Payable	900	
	Salaries Expense		900
	To reverse year-end accrual		

Jan. 4, 2008	Salaries Expense	4,500	
	Cash		4,500
	To record payment of salaries		

Posting of journalized transactions:

No reversing entries are made:	Reversing entries are made:

Cash		
	Jan. 4	4,500

Cash		
	Jan. 4	4,500

Salaries Payable		
	Dec. 31	900
Jan. 4 900		

Salaries Payable		
	Dec. 31	900
Jan. 4 900		

Salaries Expense			
Dec. 31 900	Dec. 31 900
Bal. 0	
Jan. 4 3,600	

Salaries Expense			
Dec. 31 900	Dec. 31 900
Bal. 0	
	Jan. 1 900
Jan. 4 4,500	
Bal. 3,600	

Income Summary	
Dec. 31 900*	

Income Summary	
Dec. 31 900*	

*Because this is a partial posting, the Income Summary account has not been closed since the revenue account has not been used.

Note: Whether the company uses reversing entries or does not use reversing entries, the effect on the Salaries Expense account finally comes to the same balance of $3,600 debit on January 4, 2008. This is the expense for the current period only.

Demonstration Problem (SO 1 and 4)

The newly hired accounting assistant of Courtney Jeans has produced an adjusted trial balance with the accounts balanced, but the accounts are not in order.

COURTNEY JEANS STORE
Trial Balance
July 31, 2008

	Debit	Credit
Cash	$14,150	
Accounts receivable	1,000	
Office equipment	5,550	
Store furniture	44,200	
Bank loan		$14,200
Utilities expense	800	
Supplies	500	
Accumulated amortization— office equipment		500
Accumulated amortization— store furniture		700
Salaries expense	17,000	
Rent expense	31,000	
Sales revenue		60,000
Accounts payable		1,600
Notes payable		16,100
C. William, drawings	10,000	
Prepaid insurance	500	
Supplies expense	300	
Amortization expense	1,200	
Advertising expense	6,000	
C. William, capital		39,100
	$132,200	$132,200

Instructions
(a) Calculate the net income for the month of July.
(b) Calculate the owner's equity at July 31, 2008.
(c) Prepare a classified balance sheet for Courtney Jeans Store at July 31, 2008. Assume that $2,000 of the notes payable is currently due, and the bank loan will be paid in August 2008.
(d) Journalize the closing entries.

Solution to Demonstration Problem

(a) Net Income = Revenue – Expenses
= $60,000 – $800 – $17,000 – $31,000 – $300 – $1,200 – $6,000
= $3,700

(b) Owner's equity = $39,100 + $3,700 – $10,000 = $32,800

(c)

COURTNEY JEANS STORE
Balance Sheet
July 31, 2008

Assets

Current assets			
Cash			$14,150
Accounts Receivable			1,000
Prepaid Insurance			500
Supplies			500
			$16,150
Property, plant, and equipment			
Office Equipment	5,550		
Less: Accumulated amortization	500	5,050	
Store Furniture	44,200		
Less: Accumulated amortization	700	43,500	48,550
Total assets			$64,700

Liabilities and Owner's Equity

Current Liabilities			
Bank Loan			$14,200
Accounts Payable			1,600
Notes Payable (current portion)			2,000
Total current liabilities			17,800
Long-term liabilities			
Notes Payable			14,100
Total Liabilities			31,900
Owner's equity			
C. William, Capital			32,800
Total liabilities and owner's equity			$64,700

(d)

General Journal			J1
Date	**Account Titles and Explanation**	**Debit**	**Credit**
2008	Closing entries		
Dec. 31	Sales Revenue	60,000	
	Income Summary		60,000
	To close revenue account.		
31	Income Summary	56,300	
	Salaries Expense		31,000
	Rent Expense		17,000
	Advertising Expense		6,000
	Amortization Expense		1,200
	Utilities Expense		800
	Supplies Expense		300
	To close expense accounts.		
31	Income Summary	3,700	
	C. William, Capital		3,700
	To close income summary.		
31	C. William, Capital	10,000	
	C. William, Drawings		10,000
	To close drawings to capital.		

Review Questions and Exercises

Multiple Choice

Circle the letter that best answers each of the following statements.

1. (SO 1) Closing entries are used to transfer the:
    a. temporary account balances to the Owner's Capital account.
    b. revenue accounts to the Income Summary account.
    c. expense accounts to the Income Summary account.
    d. Owner's Drawings account to the Owner's Capital account.

2. (SO 1) Journalizing and posting closing entries are:
    a. usually done at the end of every month by most companies.
    b. not a required step in the accounting cycle.
    c. closed into the Income Summary account in computerized accounting.
    d. prepared and recorded only at year end by most companies.

3. (SO 1) Balance sheet accounts are considered to be:
    a. temporary accounts.
    b. permanent accounts.
    c. capital accounts.
    d. contra accounts.

4. (SO 1) The Owner's Drawings account is a(n):
    a. expense account.
    b. revenue account.
    c. permanent account.
    d. temporary account.

5. (SO 1) J. Spencer Company's Service Revenue account has a credit balance of $12,000. The entry to close Service Revenue is:
    a. credit Service Revenue $12,000, debit Income Summary $12,000.
    b. credit Service Revenue $12,000, debit J. Spencer, Drawings $12,000.
    c. debit Service Revenue $12,000, credit J. Spencer, Drawings $12,000.
    d. debit Service Revenue $12,000, credit Income Summary $12,000.

6. (SO 1) Which of the following accounts will appear on the post-closing trial balance?
    a. Service Revenue
    b. Accumulated Amortization
    c. Amortization Expense
    d. Owner's Drawings

7. (SO 1) The number of accounts appearing in the trial balance will normally be:
    a. less than the number of accounts in the post-closing trial balance.
    b. equal to the number of accounts in the adjusted trial balance.
    c. more than the number of accounts in the post-closing trial balance.
    d. more than the number of accounts in the adjusted trial balance.

8. (SO 1) The post-closing trial balance contains only:

    a. income statement accounts.
    b. balance sheet accounts.
    c. balance sheet and income statement accounts.
    d. income statement, balance sheet, and statement of owner's equity accounts.

9. (SO 2) Which of the following statements concerning the accounting cycle is incorrect?

    a. The accounting cycle includes journalizing transactions and posting to ledger accounts.
    b. The accounting cycle includes only one optional step.
    c. The steps in the accounting cycle are performed in sequence.
    d. The steps in the accounting cycle are repeated in each accounting period.

10. (SO 2) The steps in the accounting cycle:

    a. are done in sequence beginning with step 1 in each accounting period.
    b. are not necessarily repeated in each accounting period.
    c. begin with the journalizing of transactions.
    d. can begin at any step in the cycle in each accounting period.

11. (SO 2) Which of the following statements is true?

    a. Work sheets and reversing entries are avoidable.
    b. Reversing entries and correcting entries are optional.
    c. Reversing entries are avoidable and correcting entries are optional.
    d. Work sheets and reversing entries are optional.

12. (SO 3) On September 23, Polar Company received a $350 cheque from Mike Moluf for services to be performed in the future. The bookkeeper for Polar Company incorrectly debited Cash for $350 and credited Accounts Receivable for $350. The amounts have been posted to the ledger. To correct this entry, the bookkeeper should:

    a. debit Cash $350 and credit Unearned Revenue $350.
    b. debit Accounts Receivable $350 and credit Unearned Revenue $350.
    c. debit Accounts Receivable $350 and credit Cash $350.
    d. debit Accounts Receivable $350 and credit Service Revenue $350.

13. (SO 3) On June 19, the Pinkowski Company bought office supplies on account from the Ewell Company for $550. Pinkowski Company incorrectly debited Office Equipment for $500 and credited Accounts Payable for $500. The entries have been posted to the ledger. The correcting entry is:

a. Office Supplies	550	
Accounts Payable		550
b. Office Supplies	550	
Accounts Payable		500
Office Equipment		50
c. Office Supplies	550	
Office Equipment		550
d. Office Supplies	550	
Office Equipment		500
Accounts Payable		50

14. (SO 4) Which of the following accounts is not classified under the current asset section of the balance sheet?

    a. Prepaid Expenses
    b. Supplies
    c. Equipment
    d. Cash

15. (SO 4) Which of the following statements about current assets is correct?

    a. The time period for current assets is within one year after the balance sheet date.
    b. The time period for current assets is within the year of the balance sheet date.
    c. Current assets are currently due as the company makes sales.
    d. Current assets are listed on the balance sheet in order of magnitude.

16. (SO 4) Long-term investments are:

    a. reported on the balance sheet after intangible assets.
    b. resources that are not expected to be realized in cash within one year.
    c. resources that are intended for use or consumption.
    d. resources that may include rights and privileges granted by government authorities.

17. (SO 4) Which of the following statements is true of property, plant, and equipment?

    a. They are tangible resources that are for sale.
    b. They are all reported on the balance sheet at cost less accumulated amortization.
    c. They include long-lived, non-physical resources such as patents and copyrights.
    d. They include land, buildings, equipment, and machinery.

18. (SO 4) Current liabilities:

    a. are expected to be paid from existing current assets or through the creation of other current liabilities in the coming year.
    b. are listed on the balance sheet in order of their expected maturity.
    c. might not be paid within one year depending on the company's liquidity.
    d. should not include long-term debt that is expected to be paid within the next year.

19. (SO 5) Liquidity is the measurement of:

    a. how much cash a company has at a certain date.
    b. how many sales are made on a cash basis during the reporting period.
    c. a company's ability to pay its debts as they come due.
    d. a company's ability to retain cash for payments to the owners of the business.

20. (SO 5) Working capital is a measure of liquidity and is calculated using:

    a. current liabilities – current assets expressed as a ratio.
    b. current assets – current liabilities expressed in a dollar amount.
    c. current assets – current liabilities expressed as a ratio.
    d. current liabilities – current assets expressed as a dollar amount.

*21.(SO 6) Which of the following is not a column heading on a work sheet?

  a. Trial balance

  b. Income statement

  c. Post-closing trial balance

  d. Adjusted trial balance

*22.(SO 6) Which of the following account balances is extended to the income statement columns on a work sheet?

  a. Prepaid Insurance

  b. Unearned Revenue

  c. Amortization Expense

  d. Accumulated Amortization

*23.(SO 7) Malikowski Company had accrued salaries between September 15 and September 30 of $6,000 that will be paid on October 5. The appropriate adjusting entry was made at year end, September 30. If a reversing entry is made on October 1, the entry would be:

  a. debit Salaries Payable $6,000 and credit Salaries Expense $6,000.

  b. credit Salaries Payable $6,000 and debit Salaries Expense $6,000.

  c. debit Salaries Payable $6,000 and credit Income Summary $6,000.

  d. credit Salaries Payable $6,000 and debit Income Summary $6,000.

*24.(SO 7) On November 1, 2008, Nillson Company issued a $12,000, 8 percent, three-month note payable to Barshinger Bank. On December 31, 2008, Nillson Company's year end, Nillson made the appropriate adjusting entries and, on January 1, 2009, Nillson Company made the correct reversing entries. On January 30, 2009, Nillson paid Barshinger Bank the amount of the note payable plus the interest. The entry on January 30, 2009 is:

a. Notes Payable	12,000	
Cash		12,000
b. Notes Payable	12,000	
Interest Expense	240	
Cash		12,240
c. Notes Payable	12,000	
Interest Payable	160	
Interest Expense	80	
Cash		12,240
d. Notes Payable	12,000	
Interest Payable	240	
Cash		12,240

*25.(SO 7) When reversing entries are used compared to when reversing entries are not used for salaries expense:

  a. the closing entries are different.

  b. the subsequent entry to the Salaries Expense account is the same.

  c. the balance in the Salaries Expense account after the first payment of salaries in the new period is the same.

  d. the first payment of cash for salaries in the new period is different.

Matching

Match each term with its definition by writing the appropriate letter in the space provided.

Terms	Definitions
____ 1. Reversing entry	a. A listing of the accounts and their balances after closing entries have been journalized and posted.
____ 2. Income summary	b. Cash and other assets that are reasonably expected to be realized in cash or sold or consumed in the business within one year of the balance sheet date.
____ 3. Work sheet	
____ 4. Property, plant, and equipment	c. The ability of a company to meet obligations expected to come due in the next year.
____ 5. Current liabilities	d. Non-current resources that do not have physical substance.
____ 6. Intangible assets	e. Entries made when errors are discovered.
____ 7. Classified balance sheet	f. Entries at the end of the accounting period that transfer each temporary account balance to the permanent Owner's Equity account.
____ 8. Long-term liabilities	g. Resources that can be realized in cash, but conversion is not expected within one year.
____ 9. Current assets	h. The exact reverse of an adjusting entry.
____ 10. Liquidity	i. A multiple-column form that may be used in the adjustment process and in preparing financial statements.
____ 11. Closing entries	j. A balance sheet that contains significant subgroups.
____ 12. Long-term investments	k. An account that is used in the closing process.
____ 13. Post-closing trial balance	l. Obligations expected to be paid after one year.
____ 14. Correcting entries	m. Obligations that are reasonably expected to be paid from existing current assets or through the creation of other current liabilities within the next year.
	n. Resources of a relatively permanent nature that are being used in the business and are not intended for sale.

Exercises

E4-1   (SO 1) The adjusted trial balance for Jazz Company at December 31, 2008, follows:

JAZZ COMPANY
Adjusted Trial Balance
December 31, 2008

	Debit	Credit
Cash	$ 6,000	
Accounts receivable	6,500	
Supplies	4,000	
Prepaid insurance	6,000	
Equipment	10,000	
Accumulated amortization—equipment		$ 1,000
Note payable		9,750
Unearned revenue		2,650
Interest payable		300
Salaries payable		850
K. Oliver, capital		12,000
K. Oliver, drawings	3,600	
Service revenue		24,700
Salaries expense	8,850	
Supplies expense	2,000	
Insurance expense	3,000	
Amortization expense	1,000	
Interest expense	300	
	$51,250	$ 51,250

Instructions
(a) Prepare the closing entries at December 31.
(b) Prepare a post-closing trial balance at December 31.

(a)

General Journal			JI
Date	**Account Titles and Explanation**	**Debit**	**Credit**

(b)

JAZZ COMPANY
Post-Closing Trial Balance
December 31, 2008

	Debit	Credit

*E4-2 (SO 6) Using the information provided in E4-1, complete the work sheet for Jazz Company.

JAZZ COMPANY
Work Sheet
Year Ended December 31, 2008

Account Titles	Trial Balance Dr.	Trial Balance Cr.	Adjustments Dr.	Adjustments Cr.	Adjusted Trial Balance Dr.	Adjusted Trial Balance Cr.	Income Statement Dr.	Income Statement Cr.	Balance Sheet Dr.	Balance Sheet Cr.
Cash	6,000									
Accounts receivable	4,250									
Supplies	6,000									
Prepaid insurance	9,000									
Equipment	10,000									
Note payable		9,750								
Unearned revenue		3,100								
K. Oliver, capital		12,000								
K. Oliver, drawings	3,600									
Service revenue		22,000								
Salaries expense	8,000									
Totals	46,850	46,850								
Supplies expense										
Insurance expense										
Accumulated amortization —equipment										
Amortization expense										
Interest expense										
Interest payable										
Salaries payable										
Totals										
Net income										
Totals										

E4-3 (SO 3) You have been employed as an accounting assistant for Johannas Company and your job involves preparing correcting entries. On November 30 you found and immediately corrected the following entries recorded by the previous employee:

Jul. 21	Equipment	32,000	
	Accounts payable		32,000
	To record the purchase of equipment and supplies		
Aug. 3	S. Johannas, Drawings	7,000	
	Cash		7,000
	To record payment of travel expenses		
Sep. 23	Service Revenue	4,000	
	Cash		4,000
	To record return of cash prepaid by a client		

The following information applies to the above entries:
1. On July 21 supplies in the amount of $2,000 were purchased. To date, $1,200 of the supplies have been used up.
2. The August 3 travel expenses were for a trip that Mr. Johannas took on company business.
3. On September 23 the company returned cash to a client that was previously deposited and put in the Unearned Revenue account.

Instructions
(a) Prepare the correcting entries for the company at November 30.

General Journal			JI
Date	**Account Titles and Explanation**	**Debit**	**Credit**

(b) State the effect on the income statement if correcting entries are not prepared.

_____

_____

_____

_____

E4-4   (SO 4 & 5) The post-closing trial balance for Paria Accounting Services at July 1, 2008, follows:

PARIA ACCOUNTING SERVICES
Post-Closing Trial Balance
July 1, 2008

	Debit	Credit
Cash	$ 20,950	
Supplies	2,200	
Accounts receivable	1,000	
Prepaid insurance	250	
Building	65,500	
Accumulated amortization—building		$10,000
Furniture	9,000	
Accumulated amortization—furniture		3,000
Land	50,000	
Notes payable		6,000
Accounts payable		2,700
Salaries payable		7,200
Mortgage payable		70,000
C.R. Paria, capital		50,000
	$148,900	$148,900

Additional information: The current portion of the mortgage payable is $15,000.

Instructions
(a) Prepare a classified balance sheet in proper format.

PARIA ACCOUNTING SERVICES
Classified Balance Sheet
July 1, 2008

(b)   Calculate and explain the company's current ratio.

_____

_____

_____

_____

_____

_____

_____

_____

_____

_____

_____

_____

_____

*E4-5   (SO 1, 4, & 5) Gardin Company's December 31, 2008, trial balance is as follows:

GARDIN COMPANY
Trial Balance
December 31, 2008

	Debit	Credit
Cash	$16,000	
Accounts receivable	4,500	
Prepaid insurance	2,500	
Supplies	3,000	
Equipment	41,500	
Accounts payable		$ 5,500
Unearned revenue		1,500
Notes payable		28,000
L. Gardin, capital		24,000
L. Gardin, drawings	2,500	
Revenue		16,000
Salaries expense	3,700	
Utilities expense	400	
Marketing expense	900	
Totals	$75,000	$75,000

Gardin Company needs to make year-end adjusting entries for the following:
1. Insurance expires at the rate of $100 per month.
2. There is $2,400 worth of supplies on hand at December 31.
3. The equipment was bought on January 1, 2008 and annual amortization is $2,400.
4. Interest of $2,100 has accrued on Notes Payable.
5. Unearned revenue amounted to $700 on December 31.
6. Accrued salaries are $3,200.

Instructions
(a) Prepare an adjusted trial balance.
(b) Prepare a classified balance sheet assuming $20,000 of the notes payable are long-term.
(c) Record closing entries.
(d) Prepare a post-closing trial balance.

(a)

GARDIN COMPANY
AdjustedTrial Balance
December 31, 2008

	Debit	Credit

(b)

GARDIN COMPANY
Classified Balance Sheet
December 31, 2008

(c)

General Journal			JI
Date	**Account Titles and Explanation**	**Debit**	**Credit**

(d)

GARDIN COMPANY
Post-Closing Trial Balance
December 31, 2008

	Debit	Credit

Solutions to Review Questions and Exercises

Multiple Choice

1. (a)   Temporary account balances are all transferred to the Owner's Capital account. Items (b), (c), and (d) are the process by which the temporary accounts are transferred to the Owner's Capital account.

2. (d)   Journalizing and posting closing entries are done only at year end by most companies. It is a required step in the accounting cycle. In computerized accounting, the Income Summary account is not used.

3. (b)   The drawings, revenue, and expense accounts are considered to be temporary owner's equity accounts. At the end of an accounting period, these accounts are transferred to the capital account. Not all balance sheet accounts are capital accounts (answer (c)), but all are permanent accounts.

4. (d)   The drawings account is not an expense account (answer (a)) or a revenue account (answer (b)). It is also not a permanent account (answer (c)) because it is transferred to the capital account.

5. (d)   Revenue has a normal credit balance and is closed by a debit to Revenue and a credit to Income Summary.

6. (b)   Service Revenue, Amortization Expense, and Owner's Drawings are temporary accounts that are closed at the end of the accounting period.

7. (c)   The post-closing trial balance would have the least number of accounts because it would have only the permanent accounts. The trial balance would have both the permanent and temporary accounts. The adjusted trial balance would probably have more accounts than the trial balance because it would have the same permanent and temporary accounts plus any new accounts resulting from any adjustments.

8. (b)   The post-closing trial balance contains only balance sheet accounts because income statement accounts are nominal accounts and are closed out.

9. (b)   The accounting cycle contains two optional steps: (1) the use of a work sheet and (2) the preparation of reversing entries. Each of the other statements about the accounting cycle is true.

10. (a)   The accounting cycle is done in sequence beginning with step 1 in each accounting period.

11. (d)   The work sheets and reversing entries are optional.

12. (b)   A comparison with the incorrect entry shows that both Accounts Receivable and Unearned Revenue are understated by $350. The correcting entry is therefore (b).

13. (d) The error has caused three accounts to be incorrect: Office Equipment is overstated by $500; Office Supplies is understated by $550; and Accounts Payable is understated by $50. The correcting entry is therefore (d).

14. (c) Prepaid Expenses, Supplies, and Cash are all current assets. Equipment would be classified as property, plant, and equipment.

15. (b) The time period for current assets is within the year of the balance sheet date, not after the balance sheet date as in (a). Choices (c) and (d) are both incorrect.

16. (b) Long-term investments are not expected to be realized in cash within the next year. Choice (a) is incorrect because long-term investments are reported between current assets and property, plant, and equipment. Choice (c) is incorrect because long-term investments are not expected to be used or consumed. Choice (d) is a correct statement for intangible assets.

17. (d) Property, plant, and equipment are long-lived, physical resources used in the operation of the business and are not for sale. All the other choices are untrue.

18. (a) Choice (a) correctly states the expected source of payment. Choice (b) is incorrect because current liabilities are not listed in order of maturity. Choice (c) is incorrect because the time period is definitely one year. Choice (d) is incorrect because the current portion of long-term debt should be reported under current liabilities.

19. (c) Liquidity measures a company's ability to pay its debts as they come due.

20. (b) Working capital is calculated as current assets – current liabilities and is expressed as a dollar amount.

*21. (c) The trial balance (a), income statement (b), and adjusted trial balance (d), are all columns on the work sheet. A post-closing trial balance is not presented on the work sheet.

*22. (c) Prepaid Insurance (a), Unearned Revenue (b), and Accumulated Amortization (d) are all account balances that are extended to the balance sheet columns. Amortization Expense is transferred to the income statement columns.

*23. (a) First the adjusting entry should be determined. For this transaction, the following adjusting entry would be made:

Salaries Expense   6,000
    Salaries Payable   6,000

Then, to make the reversing entry, the above adjusting entry is reversed, both the amount and the account titles.

Salaries Payable   6,000
    Salaries Expense   6,000

*24. (b) On December 31, 2008, an adjusting entry was made to accrue $160 ($12,000 x 8% x 2/12) of interest by debiting Interest Expense for $160 and crediting Interest Payable for $160. By reversing the entry after the closing entries are made, the balance in the Interest Payable account will be zero, and Interest Expense will have a credit balance of $160. Therefore, by making the entry in (b), which includes a debit to Interest Expense of $240, the correct amount of interest, $80 ($240 – $160) for January, will be shown in Interest Expense.

*25. (c) The balance in the Salaries Expense account after the first payment of salaries in the new period is the same. The closing entries are the same, the entry to the Salaries Expense account is different, and the payment of cash is the same.

Matching

1.	h	5.	m	9.	b	13.	a
2.	k	6.	d	10.	c	14.	e
3.	i	7.	j	11.	f		
4.	n	8.	l	12.	g		

Exercises

E4-1

(a)

General Journal			J1
Date	**Account Titles and Explanation**	**Debit**	**Credit**
2008	Closing entries		
	(1)		
Dec. 31	Service Revenue	24,700	
	Income Summary		24,700
	To close revenue to income summary.		
	(2)		
31	Income Summary	15,150	
	Salaries Expense		8,850
	Supplies Expense		2,000
	Insurance Expense		3,000
	Amortization Expense		1,000
	Interest Expense		300
	To close expense accounts to income summary.		
	(3)		
31	Income Summary	9,550	
	K. Oliver, Capital		9,550
	To close income summary account to capital.		
	(4)		
31	K. Oliver, Capital	3,600	
	K. Oliver, Drawings		3,600
	To close drawings to capital.		

(b)

JAZZ COMPANY
Post-Closing Trial Balance
December 31, 2008

	Debit	Credit
Cash	$ 6,000	
Accounts receivable	6,500	
Supplies	4,000	
Prepaid insurance	6,000	
Equipment	10,000	
Accumulated amortization—equipment		$ 1,000
Note payable		9,750
Unearned revenue		2,650
Salaries payable		850
Interest payable		300
K. Oliver, capital ($12,000 + $9,550 − $3,600)		17,950
	$32,500	$32,500

*E4-2

JAZZ COMPANY
Work Sheet
For the Year Ended December 31, 2008

Account Titles	Trial Balance Dr.	Trial Balance Cr.	Adjustments Dr.	Adjustments Cr.	Adjusted Trial Balance Dr.	Adjusted Trial Balance Cr.	Income Statement Dr.	Income Statement Cr.	Balance Sheet Dr.	Balance Sheet Cr.
Cash	6,000				6,000				6,000	
Accounts receivable	4,250		(e) 2,250		6,500				6,500	
Supplies	6,000			(a) 2,000	4,000				4,000	
Prepaid insurance	9,000			(b) 3,000	6,000				6,000	
Equipment	10,000				10,000				10,000	
Note payable		9,750				9,750				9,750
Unearned revenue		3,100	(d) 450			2,650				2,650
K. Oliver, capital		12,000				12,000				12,000
K. Oliver, drawings	3,600				3,600				3,600	
Service revenue		22,000		(d) 450 (e) 2,250		24,700		24,700		
Salaries expense	8,000		(g) 850		8,850		8,850			
Totals	46,850	46,850								
Supplies expense			(a) 2,000		2,000		2,000			
Insurance expense			(b) 3,000		3,000		3,000			
Accumulated amortization—equipment				(c) 1,000		1,000				1,000
Amortization expense			(c) 1,000		1,000		1,000			
Interest expense			(f) 300		300		300			
Interest payable				(f) 300		300				300
Salaries payable				(g) 850		850				850
Totals			9,850	9,850	51,250	51,250	15,150	24,700	36,100	26,550
Net income							9,550			9,550
Totals							24,700	24,700	36,100	36,100

E4-3

(a) Correcting Entries

Nov.	30	Supplies Expense	1,200	
		Supplies	800	
		Equipment		2,000
	30	Travel Expense	7,000	
		S. Johannas, Drawings		7,000
	30	Unearned Revenue	4,000	
		Service Revenue		4,000

(b) Supplies Expense not included—the expenses would have been understated, and thus income would have been overstated.

Travel Expense not included—the expenses would have been understated, and thus income would have been overstated.

Service Revenue debited—the revenue would have been understated, and thus income would have been understated.

E4-4

(a)

PARIA ACCOUNTING SERVICES
Balance Sheet
July 1, 2008

Assets

Current assets
  Cash $20,950
  Accounts receivable   1,000
  Prepaid insurance   250
  Supplies   2,200
    Total current assets   24,400

Property, plant, and equipment
  Land $50,000
  Building $65,500
  Less: Accumulated amortization   10,000   55,500
  Furniture   9,000
  Less: Accumulated amortization   3,000   6,000
    Total property, plant and equipment   111,500
      Total assets $135,900

Liabilities and Owner's Equity

Current liabilities
  Accounts payable $ 2,700
  Notes payable   6,000
  Salaries payable   7,200
  Mortgage payable (current portion)   15,000
    Total current liabilities   30,900
Long-term liabilities
  Mortgage payable (minus current portion)   55,000
    Total liabilities   85,900
Owner's equity
  C.R.Paria   50,000
    Total liabilities and owner's equity $135,900

(b) Current ratio   = current assets ÷ current liabilities
                = $24,400 ÷ $30,900
                = 0.79:1

The current ratio is a measure of the liquidity of the company. It measures the company's ability to pay debt that is due within the next year with its current assets. For every $1.00 of current debt, this company has $0.79 of current assets. This company might have difficulty paying its current debt.

E4-5
(a)

GARDIN COMPANY
Adjusted Trial Balance
December 31, 2008

Account Titles	Trial Balance Dr.	Trial Balance Cr.	Adjustments Dr.	Adjustments Cr.	Adjusted Trial Balance Dr.	Adjusted Trial Balance Cr.
Cash	16,000				16,000	
Accounts receivable	5,200				4,500	
Prepaid insurance	2,500			(a) 1,200	1,300	
Supplies	3,000			(b) 600	2,400	
Equipment	40,800				41,500	
Accounts payable		5,500				5,500
Unearned revenue		1,500	(e) 800			700
Notes payable		28,000				28,000
L. Gardin, capital		24,000				24,000
L. Gardin, drawings	2,500				2,500	
Revenue		16,000		(e) 800		16,800
Salaries expense	3,700		(f) 3,200		6,900	
Utilities expense	400				400	
Marketing expense	900				900	
Totals	75,000	75,000				
Insurance expense			(a) 1,200		1,200	
Supplies expense			(b) 600		600	
Amortization expense			(c) 2,400		2,400	
Accumulated amort. equip.				(c) 2,400		2,400
Interest expense			(d) 2,100		2,100	
Interest payable				(d) 2,100		2,100
Salaries payable				(f) 3,200		3,200
Totals			10,300	10,300	82,700	82,700

(b)

GARDIN COMPANY
Balance Sheet
December 31, 2008

Assets

Current assets
Cash	$16,000
Accounts receivable	4,500
Prepaid insurance	1,300
Supplies	2,400
Total current assets	24,200

Property, plant, and equipment
Equipment	$41,500	
Less: Accumulated amortization	2,400	39,100
Total assets		$63,300

Liabilities and Owner's Equity

Current liabilities
Notes payable (current portion)	$ 8,000
Accounts payable	5,500
Salaries payable	3,200
Interest payable	2,100
Unearned revenue	700
Total current liabilities	19,500

Long-term liabilities
Notes payable	20,000
Total liabilities	39,500

Owner's equity
L. Gardin, capital	23,800*
Total liabilities and owner's equity	$63,300

*L. Gardin, capital: $24,000 less drawings of $2,500 plus net income $2,300.

(c)

General Journal			JI
Date	**Account Titles and Explanation**	**Debit**	**Credit**
2008	Closing entries		
Dec. 31	Revenue	16,800	
	Income Summary		16,800
	To close the Revenue account.		
31	Income Summary	14,500	
	Salaries Expense		6,900
	Utilities Expense		400
	Marketing Expense		900
	Insurance Expense		1,200
	Supplies Expense		600
	Amortization Expense		2,400
	Interest Expense		2,100
	To close the expense accounts.		
31	Income Summary	2,300	
	L. Gardin, Capital		2.300
	To close the Income Summary account.		
31	L. Gardin, Capital	2,500	
	L. Gardin, Drawings		2,500
	To close drawings to capital.		

(d)

GARDIN COMPANY
Post-Closing Trial Balance
December 31, 2008

	Debit	Credit
Cash	16,000	
Accounts receivable	4,500	
Prepaid insurance	1,300	
Supplies	2,400	
Equipment	41,500	
Accumulated amort. equip.		2,400
Accounts payable		5,500
Salaries payable		3,200
Interest payable		2,100
Unearned revenue		700
Notes payable		28,000
L. Gardin, capital		23,800
Totals	65,700	65,700

chapter 5
Accounting for Merchandising Operations

study objectives >>

After studying this chapter, you should be able to:

1. Describe the differences between service and merchandising companies.
2. Prepare entries for purchases under a perpetual inventory system.
3. Prepare entries for sales under a perpetual inventory system.
4. Perform the steps in the accounting cycle for a merchandising company.
5. Prepare multiple-step and single-step income statements.
6. Calculate the gross profit margin and profit margin.
7. Prepare the entries for purchases and sales of inventory under a periodic inventory system and calculate cost of goods sold (Appendix 5A).

Preview of Chapter 5

The steps in the accounting cycle for a merchandising company are the same as the steps for a service enterprise. However, merchandising companies need additional accounts and entries in order to record merchandising transactions. The chapter is organized as follows:

Merchandising Operations

study objective 1

Describe the differences between service and merchandising companies.

Measuring net income for a merchandising company is basically the same as measuring net income for a service company. The main source of revenue for the merchandising company is called **sales revenue**. Unlike the service company, expenses for a merchandising company are divided into two categories: (1) cost of goods sold and (2) operating expenses.

The **cost of goods** sold is the total cost of merchandise sold during the period. The cost of the goods sold is a major expense and is directly related to the revenue earned from the sale of goods. Sales revenue less cost of goods sold is called **gross profit**. After gross profit is calculated, operating expenses are deducted to determine net income (or loss). **Operating expenses** are expenses incurred in the process of earning revenue.

The difference between a service company and a merchandising company can be seen in the following:

Service Company	**Merchandising Company**
Service Revenue	Sales Revenue
	– Cost of Goods Sold
	= Gross Profit
– Expenses	– Operating Expenses
= Net income (loss)	= Net income (loss)

Operating Cycles

The operating cycle of a merchandising company is longer than the operating cycle of a service company. The company has to purchase the inventory before it can generate revenue by selling the inventory to customers. The time it takes to go from cash to cash in producing revenues lengthens the operating cycle of the merchandiser. Illustration 5-2 in the text shows the operating cycles for a service company and a merchandising company.

A merchandising company requires an inventory of goods to sell to its customers. For a merchandising company, inventory is an asset generally referred to as Merchandise Inventory. It is reported as a current asset on the balance sheet.

Inventory Systems

A merchandising company must keep track of its inventory to determine what is available for sale (inventory) and what has been sold (cost of goods sold). To do this, a company may use either of two systems: a perpetual or a periodic inventory system.

Perpetual Inventory System

In a perpetual inventory system, detailed records of inventory purchases and sales are maintained. All increases and decreases related to merchandise held for sale are recorded directly to the Merchandise Inventory account. The cost of goods purchased for resale is debited to the Merchandise Inventory account when purchased. The system is continuous. The use of bar codes, optical scanners, and point-of-sale software helps keep a running record of every item bought and sold.

TIP

Think of 'perpetual' as meaning 'continuous.' The inventory records are continuously being updated in a perpetual inventory system. When merchandise inventory is received, records are increased. When merchandise inventory is sold to the customer or returned to the manufacturer for refund or exchange, records are decreased. When inventory previously sold to customers is returned, inventory is increased (provided the goods can be resold).

This means that in a perpetual inventory system, the Merchandise Inventory account must be used in every journal entry that involves an increase or decrease to merchandise inventory.

Periodic Inventory System

In a periodic inventory system, detailed inventory records of goods on hand are not kept throughout the period. A physical count is taken to determine the cost of goods on hand at the end of the period. The cost of goods on hand subtracted from the goods available for sale is used to determine the cost of goods sold. This is done only at the end of an accounting period—that is, periodically.

> Beginning inventory
> – Cost of goods purchased
> = Goods available for sale
> – Ending inventory
> = Cost of goods sold

Comparisons between perpetual and periodic inventory systems are shown in Illustration 5-4 of the text.

Companies decide which system to use based on the cost of the system and the benefit to the company. Before the widespread use of computers, periodic inventory systems were widely used by companies selling thousands of low-unit-value items with rapid turnover. Perpetual inventory systems were used for high-value goods such as automobiles or major home appliances.

With computerization and the widespread use of electronic scanners and inventory software, the use of the perpetual inventory system has expanded because it has become less expensive to use. There are still some companies that use a periodic inventory system, however. For example, some small businesses may use periodic inventory systems because the cost of a detailed perpetual system outweighs the benefits for that business.

The periodic system is described in Appendix 5A in the text.

Recording Purchases of Merchandise

Purchases of inventory, whether for cash or on credit, are recorded by the buyer when goods are received from the seller. Every purchase should be supported by a business document, such as a purchase order. Cash purchases should be supported by a cash register receipt and credit purchases by a purchase invoice. Both of these documents should show relevant information about the purchase, such as the items purchased, the quantity of each item purchased, and the total purchase price.

study objective 2

Prepare entries for purchases under a perpetual inventory system.

Under a perpetual inventory system, when merchandise is purchased for resale, the current asset—Merchandise Inventory—is debited for the cost of goods purchased. Other purchases made by the business for its own use (such as supplies, equipment, and other items) should be debited to the specific asset account and not to the Merchandise Inventory account.

Subsidiary Inventory Records

A subsidiary ledger is a group of accounts that share common characteristics. It is an addition to and an expansion of the general ledger. Illustration 5-6 in the text shows the relationship of the general ledger to the subsidiary ledger. It contains individual inventory account records for each item of inventory the company owns.

The subsidiary ledger frees the general ledger from the detail of individual balances of items on hand. The general ledger account that summarizes the subsidiary ledger data is called a control account. Other control accounts in the general ledger, such as Accounts Payable and Accounts Receivable, track individual creditor and customer balances in subsidiary ledgers.

Sales Taxes

Sales taxes include the federal Goods and Services Tax (GST) and the Provincial Sales Tax (PST). In the Atlantic provinces (excluding Prince Edward Island), the Harmonized Sales Tax (HST), a combination of GST and PST, is paid on goods purchased.

GST is paid by merchandising companies on the goods purchased for resale. The GST does not form part of the merchandise purchased because GST on items purchased is offset by GST paid on items sold. PST is not paid by merchandising companies on goods purchased for resale; PST is paid by the final consumer. Accounting for sales taxes is explained in Appendix B of the textbook.

Freight Costs

Freight cost is the transportation cost of goods from the seller's to the buyer's place of business. Freight terms (i.e., who will assume the risk for the goods during transit) are outlined in the purchase agreement. Terms are expressed F.O.B. shipping point or F.O.B. destination. F.O.B. means "free on board."

F.O.B. shipping point means that the buyer accepts ownership when the goods are placed on the carrier by the seller, and the buyer pays the freight costs and is responsible for any damages to the goods. F.O.B. destination means that the buyer accepts ownership when the goods are delivered to the buyer's place of business, and the seller pays the freight and is responsible for damages.

Any freight paid by the buyer becomes part of the cost of the merchandise purchased; Merchandise Inventory is debited for the freight costs. As an example, assume that on June 12 Caprice Retail Company bought $4,300 of inventory from General Wholesale Company on credit, F.O.B. shipping point. The inventory is delivered by Ace Delivery Company to Caprice Retail on June 12. Caprice pays $120 cash for freight charges. The entry to record freight cost is:

Jun. 12	Merchandise Inventory	120	
	Cash		120
	To record payment of freight charges		

Purchase Returns and Allowances

When a buyer is dissatisfied with merchandise because of damage, defect, inferior quality, or failure to meet the buyer's specifications, the buyer may return the goods to the seller. Sometimes the buyer chooses to keep the merchandise if the seller grants an allowance (deduction) from the purchase price.

These transactions are called purchase returns and purchase allowances. If the purchase was made for cash, the buyer would receive a cash refund; if the purchase was made on account, the seller would issue a credit memorandum. For the buyer, purchase returns and allowances are recorded as a credit to the Merchandise Inventory account. In both cases, the result is a decrease in the cost of goods purchased.

Assume that on June 15 Caprice Retail returns $300 worth of merchandise to General Wholesale. The goods had originally been bought on account. The entry to record the return of unsuitable or damaged inventory is:

Jun. 15	Accounts Payable	300	
	Merchandise Inventory		300
	To record return of goods to General Wholesale		

Discounts

Purchase discounts may be offered to customers for early payment of the balance due. The credit terms might be stated as 1/10, n/30. This means that a 1 percent cash discount may be taken on the invoice price if payment is made within 10 days of the invoice date (the discount period), otherwise the full invoice price is due 30 days from the invoice date.

Assume that Caprice Retail's $4,300 purchase of inventory from General Wholesale Co. was on credit and the terms were 1/10, n/30. The invoice date was June 12. On June 19 the balance owing to General Wholesale is $4,000 ($4,300 – $300). The entry to record Caprice's payment on June 19 is:

Jun. 19	Accounts Payable	4,000	
	Merchandise Inventory ($4,000 x 1%)		40
	Cash		3,960
	To record payment made within discount period		

Quantity discounts, where sellers give a reduction in price when inventory is purchased in large quantities, are not the same as purchase discounts. They are not recorded or accounted for separately. If a quantity discount is offered, the net purchase price (after deducting the discount) is recorded as a debit to Merchandise Inventory. The inventory will be recorded at the actual cost.

Assume that General Wholesale sells 1,000 ladies pants to Caprice Retail and the price per item is $10. However, the seller has offered a quantity discount of 20 percent on orders of 1,000 to 1,500 items. Caprice's total invoice would be $8,000 ([1,000 x $10] x 80%). The entry to record the purchase on June 25 is:

Jun. 25	Merchandise Inventory	8,000	
	Cash		8,000

Most companies take advantage of discounts offered by sellers. It reduces the amount of money companies have to pay out and allows them to use the cash for other purposes.

Summary of Purchase Transactions

Using a T account, the effect of the purchase return and the purchase discount on the goods originally purchased by Caprice Retail on June 12 follows:

Merchandise Inventory			
Jun. 12 (Purchase)	4,300	Jun. 15 (Return)	300
Jun. 12 (Freight)	120	Jun. 19 (Discount)	40
Bal.	4,080		

Recording Sales of Merchandise

Sales revenue is recorded when it is earned in accordance with the revenue recognition principle. This typically happens when goods are transferred from the seller to the buyer. Sales may be for cash or on credit.

study objective 3

Prepare entries for sales under a perpetual inventory system.

There are two journal entries being recorded for each sale in a perpetual inventory system. Assume, for example, that a retail company buys 100 T-shirts for $1,000 on July 1. On July 3 the 100 T-shirts were all sold for a total of $5,000 with terms 1/10, n/30. The entries for the sale of the T-shirts would be as follows:

Jul. 3	Accounts Receivable	5,000	
	Sales		5,000
	To record the sale of merchandise		

Jul. 3	Cost of Goods Sold	1,000	
	Merchandise Inventory		1,000
	To record the cost of merchandise sold		

> **TIP**
> Do not confuse the selling price of the goods with the purchase price (cost of goods sold). A merchandising company must achieve a profit from the sale of inventory. Be sure that the number you have recorded as a credit to sales (revenue) is greater than the number you have recorded as a debit to cost of goods sold (expense).

The recording of transactions using the perpetual inventory system does two things: there is an immediate matching of sales revenue to cost of the goods sold, and the company's inventory is immediately updated.

Some merchandisers use more than one sales account. These sales accounts give details on individual sales accounts and are used internally. For external purposes, one sales figure might be used so that details of sales are not known by competitors.

Sales Taxes

Sales taxes collected on goods sold by the merchandiser are recorded in a liability account because they are collected on behalf of the federal and provincial governments and must be paid to them periodically. Sales taxes are not recorded as revenue. Until the tax is paid to the government, it is a liability to the company. When the taxes are remitted to the government, the liability is reduced by a debit and cash is credited.

Accounting for sales taxes is explained in Appendix B of the textbook.

Freight Costs

Freight costs incurred by the seller on outgoing merchandise are an operating expense. As discussed earlier, the term F.O.B. destination means that the seller is responsible for the shipping costs.

These costs are debited to a Freight Out or Delivery Expense account if they are identified separately. When the seller pays the freight charges, they will usually set a higher invoice price for the goods to cover the expense of shipping.

Sales Returns and Allowances

Sales returns and allowances result when a customer is dissatisfied with merchandise and returns the goods to the seller for a refund or when the seller is willing to grant an allowance (deduction) from the selling price.

The effect of the sales returns and allowances on sales is a reduction of sales. Items that are not damaged are returned to inventory, thus reducing the cost of goods sold. However, it is important for management to know the amount of sales returns and allowances. These amounts are kept in a separate account, making it easy for management to analyze the account and find reasons for returns and allowances.

The information in the Sales Returns and Allowances account is important to management, who is looking for inefficiencies in the business. The use of Sales Returns and Allowances avoids a direct debit to Sales, which would distort comparisons of total sales in different accounting periods.

Assume that on July 4, two T-shirts sold on credit for $50 each were returned by the customer. The items originally cost the seller $10 each. The items were returned to the seller's inventory. The entry to record the sales return is:

Jul. 4	Sales Returns and Allowances	100	
	Accounts Receivable		100
	Merchandise Inventory	20	
	Cost of Goods Sold		20

This first entry accounts for the return of the item and the fact that it was sold on credit. If it were a cash sale, the credit would have been to the Cash account. The second entry is done if the item returned can be resold. Sales Returns and Allowances is a contra revenue account and the normal balance of the account is a debit.

Discounts

Quantity discounts and sales discounts affect both the seller and the buyer. No separate entry is made to record a quantity discount; the sale is recorded at the volume discount price.

The seller may offer the customer a cash discount for prompt payment of the balance due. To record the cash discount, a Sales Discount account is used instead of debiting Sales. This account is a contra revenue account with a normal debit balance. To determine net sales, the balances in the Sales Discounts and Sales Returns and Allowances accounts are both subtracted from the balance in the Sales account.

Assume that on July 10, the T-shirt company received payment for the outstanding balance. The customer took advantage of the 1 percent discount offered at the time of sale. The entry to record the payment with the discount is:

Jul. 10	Cash	4,851	
	Sales Discount ($4,900 x 1%)	49	
	Accounts Receivable ($5,000 – $100)		4,900

Summary of Sales Transactions

Using T accounts, the effect of the sales returns and allowances on the T-shirts originally sold on July 3 follows:

Sales			Sales Returns and Allowances		
	Jul.3	5,000	Jul.4	100	

Sales Discount			Cost of Goods Sold		
Jul.10	49		Jul.3	1,000	Jul.4	20

Completing the Accounting Cycle

In addition to purchase and sale transactions, there are further steps in the accounting cycle for a merchandising company, which we will consider now.

Adjusting Entries

In a perpetual inventory system, the Merchandise Inventory account balance should equal the cost of the merchandise on hand (ending inventory) at all times. The Merchandise Inventory account indicates what should be on hand; a physical count indicates what is actually there.

A physical count of inventory involves:
1. Counting units of inventory on hand for each item of inventory.
2. Applying unit costs to the total units on hand for each item of inventory.
3. Totalling the cost for each item of inventory to determine the total cost of goods on hand.

If the total dollar value of the physical count of the ending inventory balance is different from the amount in the ledger, an adjusting entry is required to update the Inventory account. For example, if on August 15 the ledger indicates a balance of $35,000 in the Inventory account and a physical count determines an ending inventory of $33,000, the following adjusting entry would be required:

Jul.15	Cost of Goods Sold	2,000	
	Inventory		2,000
	To record the difference between inventory records and physical count		

Closing Entries

For a merchandising company that uses the perpetual inventory system, all temporary accounts (revenue, expenses, and drawings) are closed. The journalizing steps are as follows:
1. All temporary accounts with credit balances are debited for their individual balances. The total is credited to the Income Summary account.
2. All temporary accounts with debit balances are credited for their individual balances. The total is debited to the Income Summary account.
3. The Income Summary account is closed to the Owner's Capital account.
4. Owner's Drawings, a temporary account that has a normal debit balance, is credited. The Owner's Capital account is debited in the same amount.

After the closing entries are posted, all temporary accounts should have zero balances. Only the permanent accounts (assets, liabilities, and owner's equity) should have balances.

> **TIP**
> Don't forget to also close the Sales Returns and Allowances, Sales Discounts, and Cost of Goods Sold accounts when closing the temporary accounts with debit balances.

Post-Closing Trial Balance

The post-closing trial balance of a merchandising company is prepared after the closing entries are posted. Only permanent accounts that have balances are listed. These accounts are never closed. The only additional account that the merchandising company has that is different from the service company is the current asset account Merchandise Inventory.

study objective 4

Perform the steps in the accounting cycle for a merchandising company.

Merchandising Financial Statements

In addition to the classified balanced sheet, two forms of income statements are widely used by merchandising companies: the multiple-step income statement and the single-step income statement.

Multiple-Step Income Statement

A multiple-step income statement shows several steps in determining net income or net loss. The main steps are as follows:

1. Net Sales: Sales returns and allowances and sales discounts are subtracted from sales to calculate net sales.
2. Gross Profit: Subtract cost of goods sold from net sales to calculate gross profit.
3. Income from Operations: Deduct operating expenses from gross profit to calculate income from operations.
4. Non-Operating Activities: Activities not related to operations are added (as other revenue) or subtracted (as other expenses) to calculate total non-operating activities.
5. Net income: Total non-operating activities are added to or subtracted from income from operations to calculate net income.

study objective 5

Prepare multiple-step and single-step income statements.

The first three steps involve the company's main activities. The last two steps are only needed if a company has non-operating activities. The income statement figures of the Columbus Company will be used to demonstrate the multiple steps. The pieces will be brought together at the end of the statement.

Net Sales

The multiple-step income statement for a merchandising company begins by presenting sales revenue. This section of the statement calculates net sales:

Sales Revenue		
Sales		$600,000
Less: Sales Returns and Allowances	$20,000	
Sales Discounts	5,000	25,000
Net Sales		575,000

The column at the extreme right gives the big picture about net sales. The total sales of $600,000 were affected by the sales returns, allowances, and discounts, which totalled $25,000, thus giving net sales of $575,000. The column on the inside provides details on the sales returns and allowances ($20,000) and the sales discounts ($5,000) given during the period. If there were no sales return, allowances, or discounts, the sales amount would be the same as the net sales amount.

Gross Profit

Net Sales	$575,000
Cost of Goods Sold	375,000
Gross Profit	200,000

This information is in the extreme right column. There is no additional information about the cost of goods sold. The balance is taken directly from the general ledger account.

Income from Operations

Gross Profit		$200,000
Operating Expenses		
Salaries expense	$53,000	
Rent expense	16,000	
Utilities expense	18,000	
Advertising expense	17,000	
Amortization expense	7,000	
Insurance expense	4,000	
Total operating expenses		115,000
Income from Operations		85,000

Again, the column at the extreme right gives the big picture. Total operating expenses ($115,000) subtracted from gross profit ($200,000) gives income from operations. The column on the inside provides details on the operating expenses by account for the period. Sometimes operating expenses are subdivided into selling expenses and administrative expenses. The selling expenses are associated with making sales (e.g., advertising). The administrative expenses are associated with general operating activities (e.g., accounting and legal expenses).

Non-Operating Activities

Non-operating activities consist of other revenues and expenses that are unrelated to the main operations of the business. It is shown in two sections: other revenues and other expenses. Items reported as other revenues include interest from notes receivable and short-term investments, dividend revenues, rent revenues (for a business whose main operations do not include property management), and gain on sale of property, plant, and equipment.

Other expenses include interest expense on notes and loans payable; casualty losses from vandalism and accidents; losses from sale of property, plant, and equipment; and losses from strikes by employees and suppliers.

Other revenues			
Dividend revenue	$ 9,000		
Gain on sale of office furniture	1,000		
Total non-operating revenues		$10,000	
Other expenses			
Interest expense	$ 2,000		
Casualty loss from fire	10,000		
Total non-operating expenses		12,000	
Net non-operating expense			2,000

The extreme right column shows that the net non-operating expense is $2,000. The middle column shows that the $2,000 consists of $10,000 of other revenues and $12,000 of other expenses. The inside column gives the details of the $10,000 of other revenues and the $12,000 of other expenses. In this illustration, the other expenses are greater than the other revenues. This amount will be subtracted from the income from operations to calculate net income.

Net Income
Net income is the final outcome of the company's operating and non-operating activities.

Income from Operations	$85,000
Net non-operating expenses	2,000
Net income	$83,000

Single-Step Income Statement

In a single-step income statement, all data are classified under two categories: revenues and expenses. The revenue category includes both operating revenues and other revenues. The expense category includes cost of goods sold, operating expenses, and other expenses. The single-step form is simple and easy to read. However, it does not give the detail and the order of presentation that the multiple-step statement requires.

Classified Balance Sheet

The classified balance sheet for a merchandising company is similar to a classified balance sheet for a service company. Merchandise Inventory is reported as a current asset. Current assets are listed in order of liquidity. Illustration 5-12 in the text shows the asset section of a classified balance sheet for a merchandising company.

Using the Information in the Financial Statements

Two ratios that measure profitability are the gross profit margin and the profit margin. Financial statement data are used to calculate these two ratios.

Gross Profit Margin

study objective 6

Calculate the gross profit margin and profit margin.

Gross profit margin is the company's gross profit expressed as a percentage of net sales. For example, a company that has net sales of $200,000 and cost of goods sold of $150,000 would have a gross profit of $50,000. In this case, the gross profit margin is:

$50,000	÷	$200,000	=	25%

The gross profit margin makes it possible for the company to compare profitability from one period to another, to the gross profit margin of competitors, and to industry averages.

Profit Margin

The profit margin measures the percentage of net income to net sales. That is, it measures the percentage of each dollar of sales that results in net income. For example, a company that has net sales of $200,000, gross profit of $50,000, and operating expenses of $35,000 has a net income of $15,000. In this case, the profit margin would be;

$15,000	÷	$200,000	=	7.5%

Again, this measurement is information that can be compared to past periods and industry averages. Based on these two ratio measurements, a company may improve its performance by increasing gross margin or by reducing expenses.

Appendix 5A

Periodic Inventory System

There is another system for accounting for inventories called the periodic inventory system. The perpetual inventory system, which has been the focus of this chapter, is the system that you are familiar with. One key difference between the two inventory systems is when the cost of goods sold is calculated. There are also other differences between the systems that are important to note.

In the periodic system, purchases of merchandise are recorded in the Purchases Expense account rather than in the Merchandise Inventory account. Also in the periodic system, purchase returns and allowances, purchase discounts, and freight in are recorded in separate accounts; in the perpetual system these are all recorded in the Merchandise Inventory account.

study objective 7

Prepare the entries for purchases and sales under a periodic inventory system and calculate cost of goods sold (Appendix 5A).

Recording Purchases of Merchandise

Assume that on September 12 a company buys merchandise that costs $5,000 for resale. The purchase is on credit and the terms are 2/10, n/30. The purchase of merchandise would be recorded as follows:

Sep. 12	Purchases	5,000	
	Accounts Payable		5,000
	To record purchases on account, terms 2/10, n/30		

Only goods bought for resale are recorded in the Purchases account. The purchases account is a temporary account and has a normal debit balance.

Freight Costs

On September 12, when the goods were delivered to the merchandiser, the cost of freight ($120) was payable in cash to the delivery service that made the delivery.

When the buyer pays the freight costs, the account Freight In is debited. The entry to record the freight cost is as follows:

Sep. 12	Freight In	120	
	Cash		120
	To record payment of freight on goods purchased		

Freight is part of the cost of goods purchased for resale. It is added to net purchases to determine the cost of goods purchased.

Purchase Returns and Allowances

When purchased goods are returned to the seller, it is recorded in the Purchase Returns and Allowances account. This is a contra account whose balance is deducted from the balance in the Purchases account to determine net purchases. For example, on September 14, $250 of the merchandise purchased on September 12 on credit was returned to the seller as unsatisfactory. The entry to record the return of the merchandise is as follows:

Sep. 14   Accounts Payable   250
                        Purchase Returns and Allowances   250
                   To record return of unsatisfactory merchandise to seller

Purchase Discounts
To record a discount on the purchase of merchandise, recall the terms of the purchase. For example, on September 20, payment was made for the merchandise bought on credit with payment terms 2/10, n/30. The entry to record the payment is as follows:

Sep. 20   Accounts Payable ($5,000 – $250)   4,750
                   Purchase Discounts ($4,750 x 2%)   95
                        Cash   4,655
                   To record payment of merchandise with the discount

Purchase Discounts is a temporary account with a normal credit balance. Like the Purchase Returns and Allowances account, it is also a contra account to purchases.

Recording Sales of Merchandise

Assume that on October 20 a merchandiser sells $4,000 worth of goods to a customer on account. The terms are 1/10, n/30. Under the periodic inventory system, the following journal entry is recorded at the time a sale is made:

Oct. 20   Accounts Receivable   4,000
                        Sales   4,000
                   To record credit sale to customer

Freight costs
Freight costs are paid by the merchandiser and are debited to Freight Out or Delivery Expense, which are both operating expense accounts. These costs will eventually be passed on to customers.

Sales Returns and Allowances
There is only one journal entry made to record the return of merchandise. Return of merchandise sold is recorded in an account called Sales Returns and Allowances, a contra account to sales. If $200 worth of goods from the October 20 sale was returned on October 24 by the customer, the entry would be:

Oct. 24   Sales Returns and Allowances   200
                        Accounts Receivable   200
                   To record the return of goods by customer

Sales Discount
If the customer pays the outstanding balance of the October 20 sale on October 28, taking advantage of the 1% discount, the entry is:

Oct. 28   Cash   3,762
                   Sales Discount   38
                        Accounts Receivable   3,800

Comparison of Entries—Perpetual versus Periodic

The main difference between the two inventory systems is the calculation of the cost of goods sold. In the perpetual inventory system, there is an account called Cost of Goods Sold. This account is updated as goods are purchased, returned to the merchandiser, or sold. In the periodic inventory system, there is no account called Cost of Goods Sold. Rather, the cost of goods sold is determined by a calculation at the end of the period. Illustration 5A-1 in the text shows the entries side by side for easy comparison.

Calculating Cost of Goods Sold

As stated above, under the periodic inventory system the cost of goods sold is determined using three steps:
1. Calculate the cost of goods purchased
2. Determine the cost of goods on hand at the beginning and end of the accounting period
3. Calculate the cost of goods sold

Cost of Goods Purchased

Four accounts are used to determine the cost of goods purchased under the periodic inventory system: Purchases, Purchase Returns and Allowances, Purchase Discounts, and Freight In. Using the account balances, the cost of goods purchased is determined as follows:

	Purchases
−	Purchase returns and allowances
−	Purchase discounts
=	Net purchases
+	Freight In
=	Cost of goods purchased

Cost of Goods on Hand

To determine the inventory on hand, a company must take a physical inventory where the following actions are taken:
1. Count the units on hand for each inventory item.
2. Apply the unit cost to the total units on hand for each item of inventory.
3. Total the cost of each inventory item to determine the cost of goods on hand.

The following table illustrates the calculation of the cost of goods on hand.

Item #	#11	#34	#56	#78	#99	#101	Total Inventory
Units on hand	89	100	300	300	150	76	1,015
Cost per unit	$3.00	$5.00	$6.00	$7.60	$9.00	$5.50	N/A
Totals	$267	$500	$1,800	$2,280	$1,350	$418	$6,615

Cost of Goods Sold

Calculating the cost of goods sold involves two steps:
1. Add the cost of goods purchased to the cost of goods on hand at the beginning of the period (beginning inventory). The result is the cost of goods available for sale.
2. Subtract the cost of the goods on hand at the end of the period (ending inventory) from the cost of goods available for sale. The result is the cost of goods sold.

Beginning Inventory

Purchases
− Purchase returns and allowances
− <u>Purchase discounts</u>
= Net purchases
+ <u>Freight In</u>
= Cost of goods purchased

+ <u>Cost of goods purchased</u>
= Cost of goods available for sale
− <u>Ending inventory</u>
= <u>Cost of goods sold</u>

Once the cost of goods sold is calculated, gross profit, operating expenses, and net income can be reported in a multiple-step or single-step income statement in the same way as under the perpetual inventory system. Illustration 5A-2 in the text shows the calculation of cost of goods sold for Highpoint Electronics.

Completing the Accounting Cycle

After preparing the financial statements, closing entries and a post-closing trial balance must be done to complete the accounting cycle. In the periodic inventory system, the closing entries are the same as was done previously except for the treatment of Merchandise Inventory.

In the adjusted trial balance, the Merchandise Inventory account is reported at its beginning balance (the balance at the opening of the accounting period). During the accounting period, no entries are made to the Merchandise Inventory account.

Entries must now be made to reduce the opening Merchandise Inventory balance to zero and to enter the new Merchandise Inventory amount at the end of the accounting period. The entries are as follows:
  1. The Merchandise Inventory account is credited for its beginning inventory balance and debited to the Income Summary account:
     Income Summary
        Merchandise Inventory (beginning inventory)
  2. The Merchandise Inventory account is debited for its ending inventory balance and credited to the Income summary account:
     Merchandise Inventory (ending inventory)
        Income Summary
  3. Temporary accounts with credit balances are debited for their individual account balances, and the total is credited to the Income Summary account. For example:
     Sales
     Purchase Returns and Allowances
     Purchase Discounts
        Income Summary
  4. Temporary accounts with debit balances are credited for their individual account balances, and the total is debited to the Income Summary account. For example:
     Income Summary
        Purchases
        Sales Returns and Allowances
        Sales Discounts
        Freight In

5. The Income Summary account balance is closed to the Owner's Capital account. If there is a net income, the Owner's Capital account is increased; if there is a net loss, the Owner's Capital account is decreased.
6. The drawings account, which has a normal debit balance, is closed to the Owner's Capital account. This causes a decrease in the Owner's Capital account.

Once these entries have been journalized and posted to the general ledger, a post-closing trial balance is prepared. All the permanent accounts with balances appear in the post-closing trial balance.

Demonstration Problem (SO 5)

The following is an alphabetical list of account balances for Jerome Company at December 31, 2008.

	Debit	Credit
Accounts Payable		$9,000
Accounts receivable	$ 14,200	
Accumulated amortization—building		40,000
Accumulated amortization—equipment		19,000
Advertising expense	18,000	
Amortization expense	29,500	
Building	400,000	
Cash	15,400	
Cost of goods sold	82,600	
Equipment	95,000	
Interest expense	3,250	
Interest revenue		5,000
Land	140,000	
Loss on sale of asset	1,900	
L. Jerome, capital		225,850
L. Jerome, drawings	100,000	
Merchandise inventory	29,000	
Mortgage Payable*		460,000
Notes Payable, due March 15, 2009		10,000
Prepaid Insurance	2,500	
Rent expense	10,000	
Rental revenue		6,000
Salaries expense	29,000	
Sales		212,000
Sales returns and allowances	14,000	
Supplies expense	2,500	

* $20,000 of the Mortgage Payable is due in the current period.

Instructions
(a) Prepare a multiple-step income statement for the year ended December 31, 2008.
(b) Prepare a statement of owner's equity for the year ended December 31, 2008.
(c) Prepare a classified balance sheet at December 31, 2008.

Solution to Demonstration Problem

(a)

JEROME COMPANY
Income Statement
Year Ended December 31, 2008

Sales revenue		
Sales		$212,000
Less: Sales returns and allowances		14,000
Net sales		198,000
Cost of goods sold		82,600
Gross profit		115,400
Operating expenses		
Advertising expense	$18,000	
Amortization expense	29,500	
Salaries expense	29,000	
Supplies expense	2,500	
Rent expense	10,000	
Total operating expenses		89,000
Income from operations		26,400
Other revenue and gains		
Interest revenue	$5,000	
Rental revenue	6,000	
Total other revenue and gains	$11,000	
Other expenses and losses		
Interest expense	$3,250	
Loss on sale of asset	1,900	
Total other expenses and losses	5,150	
Net non-operating revenue		5,850
Net income		$ 32,250

(b)

JEROME COMPANY
Statement of Owner's Equity
Year Ended December 31, 2008

L. Jerome, capital January 1, 2008	$225,850
Add: Net income	32,250
	258,100
Deduct: Drawings	100,000
L. Jerome, capital, December 31, 2008	$158,100

(c)

JEROME COMPANY
Balance Sheet
At December 31, 2008

Assets

Current Assets
 Cash $ 14,200
  Accounts Receivable   15,400
  Merchandise Inventory   29,000
  Prepaid Insurance   2,500
                          61,100

Property, plant and equipment
 Land   140,000
 Building $400,000
 Less: Accumulated amortization   40,000 360,000
 Equipment $ 95,000
 Less: Accumulated amortization   19,000 76,000
Total Assets $637,100

Liabilities and Owner's Equity

Current liabilities
  Accounts payable $ 9,000
  Notes payable   10,000
  Mortgage payable   20,000
                          39,000

Long-term liabilities
  Mortgage liabilities   440,000
   Total liabilities   479,000
Owner's Equity
  L. Jerome, capital   158,100
Total liabilities and owner's equity $637,100

Review Questions and Exercises
Multiple Choice

Circle the letter that best answers each of the following statements.

1. (SO 1) A merchandising company sells goods to:

	Retailers	Wholesalers
a.	yes	yes
b.	yes	no
c.	no	yes
d.	no	no

2. (SO 1) Which of the following statements is incorrect for a merchandise company?

   a. Measuring net income is basically the same as for a service company.
   b. The cost of goods sold is the same as the cost of merchandise sold.
   c. Only operating expenses are matched to revenue in calculating net income.
   d. The operating expenses for the service company are the same as the operating expenses for the merchandiser.

3. (SO 1) In a periodic inventory system:

   a. detailed inventory records are not kept throughout the period
   b. the Cost of Goods Sold account is updated when a sale is made.
   c. the beginning inventory is subtracted from the goods available for sale to calculate the cost of goods sold.
   d. the ending inventory is added to the goods available for sale to calculate the cost of goods sold.

4. (SO 1) A company would use the perpetual inventory system:

   a. if it doesn't want to do a physical inventory count.
   b. if it has goods with a low unit cost and high volume turnover.
   c. if it has many inventory items.
   d. because the system provides the company with additional information and greater control over inventory items.

5. (SO 2) Monet Company made a purchase of merchandise on credit from Claude Corporation on August 3 for $3,000, terms n/30. On August 31, Monet makes the appropriate payment to Claude. The entry on August 31 for Monet Company is:

   a. Accounts Payable   3,000
          Cash   3,000
   b. Merchandise Inventory   3,000
          Cash   3,000
   c. Accounts Payable   3,000
          Merchandise Inventory   3,000
   d. Cash   3,000
          Accounts Payable   3,000

6. (SO 2) On August 28, Renoir Company purchased office equipment from Sisley Company for $2,375 on credit. The entry by Renoir Company is:

a. Merchandise Inventory   2,375
     Accounts Payable   2,375
b. Accounts Payable   2,375
     Merchandise Inventory   2,375
c. Office Equipment   2,375
     Accounts Payable   2,375
d. Sales   2,375
     Accounts Payable   2,375

7. (SO 2) The federal GST and the provincial PST:

a. are paid on all goods and services.
b. are paid by the final consumer.
c. are paid in all provinces as separate taxes.
d. are part of the cost of a merchandise company's purchase for resale.

8. (SO 2) Which of the following statements is incorrect about purchase discounts?

a. Sellers offer purchase discounts to receive early payment on their invoices.
b. Discounts are specified on the invoice by the use of credit terms.
c. Purchase discounts are the same as quantity discounts
d. When a discount is not offered, the maximum period for payment is specified.

9. (SO 2) Purchase discounts and sales discounts are similar in that:

a. they both offer a cash discount on payments for goods within a specified period.
b. they usually offer the discount for an indefinite period of time.
c. they are similar to quantity discounts.
d. the percentage of the discount is negotiable between the buyer and the seller at the time of payment.

10. (SO 2) Cézanne Company returned defective goods costing $5,000 to the Bazille Company on March 19 for credit. The goods were purchased March 10 on credit, terms n/30. The entry made by Cézanne Company on March 19, in receiving full credit, is:

a. Cash   5,000
     Accounts Payable   5,000
b. Accounts Payable   5,000
     Cash   5,000
c. Accounts Receivable   5,000
     Merchandise Inventory   5,000
d. Accounts Payable   5,000
     Merchandise Inventory   5,000

11. (SO 3) Which of the following is true concerning freight out?

   a. Freight out increases the Merchandise Inventory account.
   b. Freight out is not an expense to a company using the perpetual inventory system.
   c. Freight out is an operating expense.
   d. Freight out is a non-operating (other) expense.

12. (SO 3) Every credit sale should be supported by a:

	Cash Register Tape	Sales Invoice
a.	yes	yes
b.	yes	no
c.	no	yes
d.	no	no

13. (SO 3) El Greco Company made a credit sale to Rubens Company when terms were n/30. Upon payment, El Greco Company should debit Cash and credit:

   a. Sales.
   b. Sales Returns and Allowances.
   c. Accounts Receivable.
   d. None of the above.

14. (SO 3) A customer, Zurbaran, is dissatisfied with merchandise purchased for $2,000 cash from the Rembrandt Company. Rembrandt Company gives Zurbaran a cash allowance of $500. The journal entry by Rembrandt Company for the allowance will include a:

   a. debit to Sales Returns and Allowances.
   b. credit to Accounts Receivable.
   c. debit to Accounts Receivable.
   d. credit to Sales Returns and Allowances.

15. (SO 3) On July 9, Goya Company sells goods on credit to Ed Manet for $3,500, terms n/30. Goya receives payment on July 18, less the return on July 15 of goods valued at $600. The entry by Goya on July 18 is:

a.	Cash	3,500	
	Accounts Receivable		3,500
b.	Cash	3,500	
	Sales		3,500
c.	Cash	2,900	
	Accounts Receivable		2,900
d.	Cash	3,500	
	Sales Returns and Allowances		600
	Accounts Receivable		2,900

16. (SO 3) Which of the following, if any, is a contra account?

	Sales Returns and Allowances	Freight Out
a.	yes	no
b.	yes	yes
c.	no	yes
d.	no	no

17. (SO 4) The physical inventory count is an important control feature because:

    a. it indicates what is actually in the inventory.
    b. it tells exactly what inventory errors have occurred.
    c. it confirms what is in the perpetual inventory records.
    d. it provides a record of the cost of goods sold.

18. (SO 4) When a physical inventory is taken, any difference between the count and the amount in the Merchandise Inventory account is:

    a. left unadjusted until the items are located.
    b. increased to account for the difference.
    c. decreased to account for the difference.
    d. adjusted, as is necessary, to account for the difference.

19. (SO 4) The post-closing trial balance is prepared:

    a. after closing the Merchandise Inventory account.
    b. after the adjusting entries are posted.
    c. to confirm that debits equal credits in the permanent accounts.
    d. to confirm that the permanent accounts have zero balances.

20. (SO 5) Which of the following statements is incorrect about a multiple-step income statement?

    a. Operating expenses may be classified as selling and administrative expenses.
    b. There may be a section for non-operating activities.
    c. There may be a section for operating assets.
    d. There is a section for cost of goods sold.

21. (SO 5) The non-operating sections of the income statement include:

    a. rent revenue for a car rental company.
    b. other revenues and expenses unrelated to a company's main operations.
    c. sales returns and allowances and sales discounts.
    d. amortization expense and losses on sales of property, plant, and equipment.

22. (SO 5) Two categories of expenses in merchandising companies are:

    a. cost of goods sold and financing expenses.
    b. operating expenses and financing expenses.
    c. cost of goods sold and operating expenses.
    d. sales and cost of goods sold.

23. (SO 6) The calculation of gross profit for a merchandising company would not normally include an account called:

    a. Cost of Goods Sold.
    b. Freight Out.
    c. Sales Revenue.
    d. Sales Returns and Allowances.

24. (SO 6) If a company has net sales of $500,000 and cost of goods sold of $350,000, the gross profit margin is:

    a. 70%
    b. 30%
    c. 15%
    d. 100%

25. (SO 6) Gross profit does not appear:

    a. on a multiple-step income statement.
    b. on a single-step income statement.
    c. to be relevant in analyzing the operation of a merchandising company.
    d. on the income statement.

*26.(SO 7) The key difference between the periodic inventory system and the perpetual inventory system is that:

    a. no physical inventory count is taken when the perpetual inventory system is used.
    b. cost of goods sold is recorded immediately as a sale is made in the perpetual inventory system.
    c. the Merchandise Inventory account is immediately updated when a sale is made in the periodic inventory system.
    d. the purchase of merchandise for sale is recorded in the Merchandise Inventory account in the periodic inventory system.

*27. (SO 7) In the periodic inventory system, freight in cost is:

    a. an operational expense.
    b. recorded in the Purchases account.
    c. part of the cost of goods purchased.
    d. recorded in the Merchandise Inventory account.

*28. (SO 7) To determine the cost of goods purchased:

    a. beginning inventory is added to purchases.
    b. freight in is added to net purchases.
    c. purchase returns and allowances is subtracted from purchases.
    d. cost of goods sold is subtracted from ending inventory.

Matching

Match each term with its definition by writing the appropriate letter in the space provided.

Terms	**Definitions**
_____ 1. Operating expenses	a. A system in which detailed inventory records are not maintained and the cost of goods sold is determined only at the end of an accounting period by taking a physical inventory.
_____ 2. Periodic inventory system	
_____ 3. Perpetual inventory system	b. A measure of the gross profit expressed as a percentage of net sales.
_____ 4. Multiple-step income statement	c. A detailed inventory system in which the cost of each inventory item is maintained and the records continuously show the inventory that should be on hand.
_____ 5. Gross profit	
	d. Net sales less cost of goods sold.
_____ 6. Income from operations	e. A non-operating section of the income statement that shows expenses pertaining to auxiliary operations and losses unrelated to the company's operations.
_____ 7. Other revenues	
_____ 8. Single-step income statement	f. A non-operating section of the income statement that shows revenues from auxiliary operations and gains unrelated to the company's operations.
_____ 9. Profit margin	
_____ 10. Other expenses	g. Expenses that relate to general operating activities.
_____ 11. Gross profit margin	h. Cost of goods available for sale less ending merchandise inventory.
_____ 12. Cost of goods sold	i. An income statement in which numerous steps are involved before net income or net loss is reported.
	j. An income statement that shows only one step in determining net income or net loss.
	k. Net sales less cost of goods sold and operating expenses.
	l. A measure of the percentage of each dollar of sales that results in net income.

Exercises

E5-1   (SO 2 & 3) During the month of October 2008, the Canadian Fiction Merchandising Company had the following transactions:

Oct.   2   Sold $5,000 of goods to Maggie Atwood for cash. The cost of the goods was $3,000.

10   Sold goods to Margaret Laurence for $3,500 on credit, terms 1/10, n/30. The goods cost $2,100.

12   Gave a cash refund of $2,500 to Maggie Atwood because half of the goods purchased on October 2 were unsatisfactory. The goods cost $1,875 and were returned to inventory.

15   Purchased $8,000 of merchandise from Richler Company on credit, terms 2/10, n/30.

17   Received cash from Margaret Laurence in full payment of the sale on October 10.

21   Received an allowance from Richler Company of $1,000 because the goods purchased on October 15 did not meet specifications.

24   Paid Richler Company the amount due.

Instructions
Journalize the transactions above, assuming that the Canadian Fiction Merchandising Company uses a perpetual inventory system.

General Journal			J1
Date	**Account Title**	**Debit**	**Credit**

E5-2   (SO 5) Using the results of the transactions of Canadian Fiction Merchandising Company in E5-1, prepare a partial income statement for the month ended October 31, 2008, up to the gross profit of the company.

CANADIAN FICTION MERCHANDISING COMPANY
Income Statement (partial)
Month Ended October 31, 2008

E5-3   (SO 5) On December 31, 2008, the adjusted account balances of the McLean Company are as follows:

	Debits		Credits
Cash	$ 3,500	Accumulated Amortization	$ 12,000
Accounts Receivable	13,000	Accounts Payable	16,250
Merchandise Inventory	40,500	A. McLean, Capital	66,500
Equipment	70,000	Sales	505,000
A. McLean, Drawings	15,000	Interest Revenue	10,900
Sales Returns and Allowances	13,850		
Cost of Goods Sold	299,850		
Freight out	6,000		
Advertising Expense	9,500		
Sales Commissions Expense	35,000		
Office Salaries	83,000		
Utilities Expense	23,000		
Interest Expense	8,700		
Amortization Expense	4,000		

Instructions

(a) Prepare a multiple-step income statement for the year ended December 31, 2008.

McLEAN COMPANY
Income Statement
Year Ended December 31, 2008

(b) Prepare a single-step income statement for the year ended December 31, 2008.

McLEAN COMPANY
Income Statement
Year Ended December 31, 2008

E5-4   (SO 6) The Ana Street Company showed the following comparative results:

	2007	**2008**
Sales	$200,000	$250,000
Sales Returns and Allowances	36,000	45,000
Cost of Goods Sold	86,000	112,000

Instructions
Calculate the gross profit of the company using dollar values and the gross profit margin. Give your analysis of the company's performance.

_____

_____

_____

_____

_____

_____

_____

_____

_____

_____

_____

_____

_____

_____

_____

_____

_____

*E5-5   (SO 7) The Esta Guama Merchandising Company uses a periodic inventory system. The results for the six-month period ending June 30, 2008, show the following account balances:

Sales	$75,000
Purchases	30,000
Total operating expenses	12,000
Purchase returns and allowances	5,000
Merchandising inventory (ending)	4,000
Sales returns and allowances	3,500
Merchandising inventory (beginning)	2,000
Sales discounts	700
Freight in	300

Instructions
For the six months ending June 30, 2008, calculate (a) net sales, (b) cost of goods sold, and (c) net income for Esta Guama Company.

ESTA GUAMA MERCHANDISING COMPANY
Income Statement Calculations
Six Months Ended June 30, 2008

(a)

(b)

(c)

_____

_____

_____

_____

_____

*E5-6   (SO 7) The following selected information is for the Esmeralda Merchandising Company for the year ended June 30, 2008:

Accounts receivable	$ 25,000
Freight in	10,000
Freight out	7,000
Insurance expense	12,000
Interest expense	6,000
Merchandising inventory, ending	40,000
Merchandising inventory, beginning	62,000
M. Esmeralda, capital	95,000
M. Esmeralda, drawings	40,000
Mortgage payable	200,000
Purchases	300,000
Purchase discounts	1,000
Purchase returns and allowances	5,000
Property tax expense	16,000
Sales revenue	475,000
Sales returns and allowances	3,500
Sales discounts	700
Salaries expense	56,000
Unearned sales revenue	25,000
Utilities expense	10,000

Instructions

(a) Prepare a multiple-step income statement.

ESMERALDA MERCHANDISING COMPANY
Income Statement
Year Ended June 30, 2008

(b) Prepare closing entries.

General Journal			JI
Date	**Account Title**	**Debit**	**Credit**

(c) Prepare a statement of owner's equity for the year ended June 30, 2008.

ESMERALDA MERCHANDISING COMPANY
Owner's Equity Statement
Year Ended June 30, 2008

Solutions to Review Questions and Exercises

Multiple Choice

1. (a) A merchandising company sells goods to both retailers and wholesalers.

2. (c) Operating expenses and cost of goods sold are matched with revenue items in calculating the net income of the merchandiser. All the other items are true.

3. (a) Detailed inventory records are not kept throughout the period.

4. (d) A company uses a perpetual inventory system if the additional information and greater control over inventory is important. There may also be cost/benefit considerations.

5. (a) A liability for a purchase on credit is decreased and the cash account is decreased.

Accounts Payable	3,000	
Cash		3,000

6. (c) The Inventory account is used to record only the cost of goods purchased for resale. All other purchases should be debited to the account that best describes their function in the business. Thus the entry:

Office Equipment	2,375	
Accounts Payable		2,375

7. (b) Both the GST and PST are eventually paid by the final consumer. Merchandisers pay the GST on goods purchased, but it is offset against the GST they collect from customers.

8. (c) Purchase discounts are not the same as quantity discounts. Purchase discounts are offered to customers for early payment and are specified by terms such as 1/10, n/30. Quantity discounts are discounts for bulk purchases.

9. (a) Both offer cash discounts for payment of the invoice within a specified discount period.

10. (d) Purchase returns on credit for defective goods will decrease the amount of the liability and decrease the inventory.

| Accounts Payable | 5,000 | |
| Merchandise Inventory | | 5,000 |

11. (c) Freight out is a selling expense and would be classified as an operating expense on a multiple-step income statement.

12. (c) Cash register tapes support cash sales, and sales invoices support credit sales.

13. (c) The entry for receipt of a balance due from a credit sale when terms were n/30 is a debit to Cash and a credit to Accounts Receivable.

14. (a) The entry for the cash allowance of $500 will include a debit to Sales Returns and Allowances and a credit to Cash.

15. (c) Cash is debited for $2,900 and Accounts Receivable is credited for $2,900. The sales return would have been recorded at the time the goods were returned.

16. (a) Sales Returns and Allowances is a contra revenue account. Freight out is a selling expense.

17. (a) The physical inventory count indicates what is actually on hand. It does not confirm errors because we do not know if there are errors in advance of the physical count.

18. (d) After the physical count, Merchandise Inventory is adjusted as necessary. We cannot assume that the count will be less than the book value of the inventory and that the adjustment will be a decrease.

19. (c) The post-closing trial balance confirms that the permanent accounts are in balance after the temporary accounts have been closed.

20. (c) Assets are listed on the balance sheet. The income statement lists revenues and expenses.

21. (b) The non-operating sections on a multiple-step income statement include only items unrelated to the company's main operations. The other answers all include items that are part of the company's main operations.

22. (c)   Financing expense is not a category of expense. Sales is a component of revenue, not an expense.

23. (b)   Freight out would not be part of the calculation of gross profit for a merchandising company. It is a selling expense.

24. (b)   Gross profit is $150,000; $150,000 divided by $500,000 equals 30 percent.

25. (b)   Gross profit does not appear on a single-step income statement. This income statement lists all revenues and all expenses, but does not make a distinction between cost of goods sold, operating, and non-operating expenses.

*26. (b)   Cost of goods sold is recorded immediately when a sale is made if using the perpetual inventory system.

*27. (c)   Freight in is part of the cost of goods purchased.

*28. (b)   To calculate cost of goods purchased, freight in is added to net purchases.

Matching

1.	g	6.	k	11.	b
2.	a	7.	f	12.	h
3.	c	8.	j		
4.	i	9.	l		
5.	d	10.	e		

Exercises

E5-1

	General Journal		J1
Date	**Account Title**	**Debit**	**Credit**
2008			
Oct. 2	Cash	5,000	
	Sales		5,000
	Cost of Goods Sold	3,000	
	Merchandise Inventory		3,000
10	Accounts Receivable	3,500	
	Sales		3,500
	Cost of Goods Sold	2,100	
	Merchandise Inventory		2,100
12	Sales Returns and Allowances	2,500	
	Cash		2,500
	Merchandise Inventory	1,875	
	Cost of Goods Sold		1,875
15	Merchandise Inventory	8,000	
	Accounts Payable		8,000
17	Sales Discounts ($3,500 x 1%)	35	
	Cash	3,465	
	Accounts Receivable		3,500
21	Accounts Payable	1,000	
	Merchandise Inventory		1,000
24	Accounts Payable	7,000	
	Merchandise Inventory ($7,000 x 2%)		140
	Cash		6,860

E5-2

CANADIAN FICTION MERCHANDISING COMPANY
Income Statement (partial)
Month endedOctober 31, 2008

Sales revenue		
Sales ($5,000 + $3,500)		$8,500
Less: Sales returns and allowances	$2,500	
Sales discounts	35	2,535
Net sales		5,965
Cost of goods sold ($3,000 + $2,100 − $1,875)		3,225
Gross profit		$2,740

E5-3

(a)

McLEAN COMPANY
Income Statement
Year Ended December 31, 2008

Sales revenues		
Sales revenues		
Sales		$505,000
Less: Sales returns and allowances		13,850
Net sales		491,150
Cost of goods sold		299,850
Gross profit		191,300
Operating expenses		
Office salaries expense	$83,000	
Sales commissions expense	35,000	
Utilities expense	23,000	
Advertising expense	9,500	
Freight out	6,000	
Amortization expense	4,000	
Total operating expenses		160,500
Income from operations		30,800
Other revenues		
Interest revenue	$10,900	
Other expenses		
Interest expense	8,700	2,200
Net income		$ 33,000

(b)

McLEAN COMPANY
Income Statement
Year Ended December 31, 2008

Revenues
  Net sales $491,150
  Interest revenue   10,900
    Total revenues   502,050

Expenses
  Cost of goods sold $299,850
  Operating expenses   160,500
  Interest expense   8,700
    Total expenses   469,050
Net income $ 33,000

E5-4

	2007	2008
Net Sales	$164,000	$205,000
Cost of Goods Sold	86,000	112,000
Gross Profit	$ 78,000	$ 93,000
Gross Profit Margin =	$78,000 ÷ $164,000	$93,000 ÷ $205,000
	48%	45%

The gross profit has increased in dollar value from $78,000 in 2007 to $93,000 in 2008. This is an increase of $15,000, which seems good until the gross profit margin is analyzed. Gross profit margin has decreased from 48 percent in 2007 to 45 percent in 2008. The company has probably spent too much buying goods for sale and has not increased sales prices to cover that increase. If the increase in the cost of goods sold is a result of better quality merchandise, the sales price should be increased to cover the increased cost.

*E5-5

ESTA GUAMA MERCHANDISING COMPANY
Income Statement (calculations)
Six Months Ended June 30, 2008

(a)

Sales revenue
  Sales $75,000
  Less: Sales returns and allowances $ 3,500
      Sales discounts   700   4,200
  Net sales $70,800

(b)

Merchandising Inventory (beginning)		$2,000
Purchases	$30,000	
Less: Purchases returns and allowances	5,000	
Net purchases	25,000	
Add: Freight in	300	
Cost of goods purchased		25,300
Cost of goods available for sale		27,300
Less: Merchandising inventory (ending)		4,000
Cost of goods sold		$23,300

(c)

Net sales	$70,800
Cost of goods sold	23,300
Gross profit	$47,500
Operating expenses	12,000
Net income	$35,500

*E5-6

(a)

ESMERALDA MERCHANDISING COMPANY
Income Statement
Year Ended June 30, 2008

Revenue			
Sales Revenue			$475,000
Less: Sales returns and allowances		$3,500	
Sales discounts		700	4,200
Net sales			470,800
Cost of Goods Sold			
Beginning Inventory		62,000	
Purchases	$300,000		
Less: Purchase ret. and allow.	$5,000		
Purchase discounts	1,000	6,000	
Net purchases		294,000	
Add: Freight in		10,000	
Cost of goods purchased		304,000	
Goods available for sale		366,000	
Less: Ending Inventory		40,000	326,000
Gross Profit			$144,800
Operating Expenses			
Insurance expense		$12,000	
Freight out		7,000	
Property tax expense		16,000	
Salaries expense		56,000	
Utilities expense		10,000	
Total operating expenses			101,000
Income from operations			43,000
Other expenses			
Interest expense			6,000
Net Income			37,800

(b) Closing entries.

General Journal			JI
Date	**Account Title**	**Debit**	**Credit**
Jun. 30	Income Summary	62,000	
	Merchandise Inventory		62,000
	To close beginning inventory		
30	Merchandise Inventory	40,000	
	Income Summary		40,000
	To close ending inventory		
30	Sales Revenue	475,000	
	Purchase Returns and Allowances	5,000	
	Purchase Discounts	1,000	
	Income Summary		481,000
	To close temporary accounts with credit balances		
30	Income Summary	434,200	
	Sales Returns and Allowances		3,500
	Sales Discounts		700
	Purchases		300,000
	Freight In		10,000
	Insurance Expense		12,000
	Interest Expense		6,000
	Freight Out		7,000
	Property Tax Expense		16,000
	Salaries Expense		56,000
	Utilities Expense		10,000
	To close temporary accounts with debit balances		
30	Income Summary	37,800	
	M. Esmeralda, Capital		37,800
	To close Income Summary to Owner's Capital		
30	M. Esmeralda, Capital	40,000	
	M. Esmeralda, Drawings		40,000
	To close drawings account to Owner's Capital.		

(c)

ESMERALDA MERCHANDISING COMPANY
Statement of Owner's Equity
Year Ended June 30, 2008

M. Esmeralda, capital, July 1, 2007	$95,000
Add: Net Income	37,800
	132,800
Deduct: Drawings	40,000
M. Esmeralda, capital, June 30, 2008	$92,800

chapter 6
Inventory Costing

Preview of Chapter 6

Accounting for inventory items can be time-consuming and complex. The procedures for determining inventory quantities, and the cost flow assumptions for determining the cost of goods sold and the cost of inventory on hand will be explained. We will also discuss the effects of inventory errors and cost flow assumptions on a company's financial statements. The chapter is organized as follows:

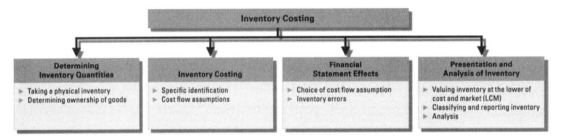

Determining Inventory Quantities

Inventory quantities are determined in two steps: (1) taking a physical inventory of goods on hand, and (2) determining the ownership of goods. The number of units of inventory owned by the company and the cost assigned to the units must be known before financial statements are prepared.

Taking a Physical Inventory

study objective 1

Describe the steps in determining inventory quantities.

A physical inventory involves actually counting, weighing, or measuring each kind of inventory on hand. It is an enormous task and is usually done when the business is closed or when business is slow. The count is usually more accurate when goods are not being sold or received during the time that the count is being done.

Taking physical inventory is an internal control procedure. Some internal control procedures for counting inventory are as follows:
1. The count should be done by employees who are not responsibile for either custody of the inventory or keeping inventory records.
2. Each counter should establish that the inventory items exist, how many of the items are on hand, and the condition of the items.
3. The count of one employee should be verified by a second employee or auditor.
4. Pre-numbered inventory tags should be used to tag items already counted so that no items are counted more than once.

Determining Ownership of Goods

Before calculating the cost of the inventory, it is necessary to consider ownership of goods. The company must be sure that it has not included any goods that do not belong to the company, or forgotten to include any goods that do belong to the company.

Goods in Transit
Goods are in transit when they are in the hands of a public carrier (railway, airline, trucking, or shipping company). Since goods in transit are not physically present when a physical inventory count is conducted, it becomes necessary to determine who has ownership of the goods in transit.

Legal title to (ownership of) goods in transit is determined by the terms of sale. Common shipping terms were discussed in Chapter 5, but are recapped below:

1. **F.O.B. shipping point:** Legal title to the goods passes to the buyer when the public carrier accepts the goods from the seller.
2. **F.O.B. destination:** Legal title to the goods remains with the seller until the goods reach the buyer.

These terms are important in determining the exact date for recording a purchase or sale of inventory and what items should be included in the financial statements. If the shipping terms are F.O.B. shipping point, the buyer has legal title to the goods in transit. If the terms are F.O.B. destination, the seller has legal title to the goods in transit.

Consigned Goods

Under a consignment arrangement, the holder of the goods (called the consignee) does not actually own the goods. The goods belong to other parties and are sold by the consignee for a fee. Ownership remains with the other party who own the goods (the consignor) until the goods are actually sold to a customer. Consigned goods should be included in the consignor's inventory. They are not to be counted in the consignee's inventory.

Other Situations

Goods taken by a customer on approval belong to the seller and should be included in the physical count of inventory. When goods are sold, but are held by the seller for pick up, delivery, or alterations, they should not be included in the inventory count.

Damaged or unsaleable goods should be separated from the physical count of inventory and the loss should be recorded.

Summary

1. Goods purchased that are in transit, shipped F.O.B. shipping point.   Include in buyer's inventory.
2. Goods purchased that are in transit, shipped F.O.B. destination.   Exclude from buyer's inventory.
3. Goods sold that are in transit, shipped F.O.B. shipping point.   Exclude from seller's inventory.
4. Goods sold that are in transit, shipped F.O.B. destination.   Include in seller's inventory.
5. Goods that are held on consignment.   Exclude from consignee's inventory.
6. Goods that are shipped on approval.   Include in seller's inventory.
7. Damaged or unsaleable goods.   Exclude from inventory (record as a loss).

Inventory Costing

After the quantity of units of inventory has been determined, unit costs are applied to the quantities to determine the total cost of the goods sold and the cost of the ending inventory. More often than not, the units purchased and recorded in the inventory have been purchased at different costs during the period.

study objective 2

Calculate ending inventory and cost of goods sold in a periodic inventory system using inventory cost flow assumptions.

It is now necessary to decide which costs should be placed on those units. These costs would be allocated to both the cost of goods sold and the ending inventory. The cost of the inventory must be allocated in a consistent and rational way. Cost is the primary basis of accounting for inventories, in keeping with the cost principle. One allocation method—specific identification—uses the actual physical flow of goods to determine cost.

Specific Identification

The specific identification method tracks the actual physical flow of the goods. Each inventory item is marked, tagged, or coded with its specific unit cost. Items left in inventory at the end of the period are specifically costed to determine the total cost of the ending inventory.

Specific identification is a practical method when a limited number of high-unit-cost items are identified from purchase through to sale. This method reports ending inventory at actual cost and matches the cost of goods sold against sales revenue. Automobiles are a good example of a type of inventory that works well with specific identification, because the dealership can identify each automobile sold by its serial number.

However, the automobile dealership may have difficulty in identifying all the different parts that are sold in the parts department. With low-unit-cost items, such as auto parts, it may be impossible or impractical to track each item individually. Therefore, it is necessary to make assumptions about the cost of units sold.

Even though bar coding has made it possible to identify nearly any type of product, there are still situations where inventory assumptions are used. At a time when the costs of commodities are rising, the cost cannot be easily tracked by the seller. For example, when crude oil prices are rising, the cost of an individual barrel of oil cannot be easily determined. The seller in this case must use a cost flow assumption to determine the cost of each barrel of crude oil it sells.

Cost Flow Assumptions

Cost flow assumptions are allowed when specific identification of items is impossible or impractical. Cost flow assumptions may be unrelated to the physical flow of goods. Three commonly used cost flow assumptions are:
1. First-in, first-out (FIFO)
2. Average cost
3. Last-in, first-out (LIFO)

Any of these cost flow assumptions can be applied in a perpetual inventory system or a periodic inventory system. The cost flow assumptions are illustrated using the periodic inventory system, where costs are allocated to ending inventory and goods sold at the end of the accounting period. Cost flow assumptions under a perpetual inventory system are explained in Appendix 6A of the textbook.

The following information will be used to illustrate inventory cost assumption methods:

Guyeri Company has the following inventory purchases data for the month of November 2008.

Date	Explanation	Units	Unit Cost	Total Cost
Nov. 1	Beg. Inventory	100	$12	$ 1,200
Nov. 5	Purchase	200	13	2,600
Nov. 15	Purchase	300	14	4,200
Nov. 24	Purchase	400	15	6,000
		1,000		$14,000

The company uses a periodic inventory system. The physical inventory count on November 31 shows 600 units on hand.

FIFO

The first-in, first-out (FIFO) cost flow assumption often matches the actual physical flow of merchandise. Selling the oldest units first is good business practice.

Under this assumption, the earliest units purchased are the first to be sold and, thus, are accounted for as the cost of goods sold. The most recently purchased units remain on hand and are accounted for as the ending inventory. Remember, this is an assumption and it does not mean that the actual first units purchased are the first units sold. There is no accounting requirement that the cost flow assumption match the actual movement of the goods.

FIFO:
Ending inventory:

Date	Units	Unit Cost	Total Cost
Nov. 24	400	$15	$6,000
Nov. 15	200	14	2,800
Total	600		$8,800

Cost of goods sold:

Cost of goods available for sale	$14,000
Less: Ending inventory	8,800
Cost of goods sold	$ 5,200

Proof of cost of goods sold:
   1,000 units available for sale – 600 in ending inventory = 400 units sold.

Date	Units	Unit Cost	Total Cost
Nov. 1	100	$12	$1,200
Nov. 5	200	13	2,600
Nov. 15	100	14	1,400
Total	400		$5,200

Average Cost

The average cost flow assumption assumes that the cost of an item is the average price of all goods available for sale. Under this assumption, the allocation of the cost of goods available for sale is made on the basis of weighted-average unit cost incurred, not just a simple average. The formula for determining the weighted-average unit cost is cost of goods available for sale divided by total units available for sale.

Weighted-average unit cost:

Cost of goods available for sale	÷	Total units available for sale	=	Weighted-average unit cost
$14,000	÷	1,000	=	$14.00

Ending Inventory:
   = $14.00 x 600 units = $ 8,400

Cost of good sold:

Cost of goods available for sale	$14,000
Less: Ending inventory	8,400
Cost of goods sold	$ 5,600

Proof of cost of goods sold:
   $14.00 x 400 units = $5,600

LIFO

The LIFO cost flow assumption seldom coincides with the actual physical flow of inventory. Under this assumption, all goods purchased during the period are assumed to be available for sale, regardless of the date of purchase. The most recently purchased units are the first to be sold. The earliest units purchased remain on hand and are the ending inventory.

LIFO:
Ending inventory:

Date	Units	Unit Cost	Total Cost
Nov. 1	100	$12	$1,200
Nov. 5	200	13	2,600
Nov. 15	300	14	4,200
Total	600		$8,000

Cost of goods sold:

Cost of goods available for sale	$14,000
Less: Ending inventory	8,000
Cost of goods sold	$ 6,000

Proof of cost of goods sold:

Date	Units	Unit Cost	Total Cost
Nov. 24	400	$15	$6,000

TIP

For each cost flow assumption, the value of the cost of goods sold added to the value of the ending inventory must be equal to the total cost of the goods available for sale for the period.

	Cost of goods sold	+	Ending inventory	=	Cost of goods available for sale
FIFO	$ 5,200	+	$8,800	=	$14,000
Average	5,600	+	8,400	=	14,000
LIFO	6,000	+	8,000	=	14,000

Financial Statement Effects

study objective 3

Determine the effects of the inventory cost flow assumptions and inventory errors on the financial statements.

Companies can use all three cost flow assumptions and specific identification. A company may also use different cost flow assumptions for inventories with a different nature or use. Only a few Canadian companies use LIFO. Those who use LIFO usually do it to harmonize their reporting practices with U.S. companies where LIFO is used more often. At the time of writing this Study Guide, new Canadian standards disallowing LIFO have been proposed.

FIFO and average cost flow assumptions are more popular in Canada. Whichever cost flow assumption is used, the same assumption or assumptions must be used from one reporting period to the next. This ensures that the statements are consistent, so they can be compared from period to period.

Companies may change the cost flow assumptions used. However, the company must disclose the change and its effect on net income. When companies adopt different inventory cost flow assumptions, they must go back and restate the prior year's financial statements using the new method. The full disclosure principle requires all relevant information be disclosed.

Income Statement Effects
In periods of changing prices, the choice of cost flow assumption can have a significant impact on net income. Remember that the allocation of cost of goods sold affects income. In periods of rising prices, FIFO reports the highest net income, LIFO the lowest, and average cost falls in the middle. The reverse is true when prices are falling. If prices are stable, all three cost flow assumptions will report the same results.

LIFO provides the best income statement valuation. It matches current costs with current revenue since the cost of goods sold is assumed to be the cost of goods most recently acquired.

Balance Sheet Effects
Cost flow assumptions affect the balance sheet because the ending inventory is an asset on the balance sheet. FIFO produces the best balance sheet valuation since in a period of rising prices, the cost of the ending inventory will approximate the inventory's current or replacement cost. Under LIFO, the ending inventory is much lower than the current cost of replacing the inventory.

Summary of Effects
Revenue and purchases are not affected by the choice of cost flow assumption. However, the cost of goods sold and the ending inventory will be affected by the cost flow assumptions and so will have an effect on net income. All three cost flow assumptions will have the same impact on pre-tax cash flow and will give exactly the same results over the life cycle of the business or its product.

Inventory Errors

Inventory errors may occur in taking or costing the inventory. They may be caused by incorrect inventory counting or pricing, or sometimes because of improper recognition of the transfer of legal title for goods in transit.

Income Statement Effects
The cost of goods available for sale (beginning inventory plus cost of goods purchased) is allocated between cost of goods sold and ending inventory. An error in any one of these components will affect the income statement and the balance sheet. The dollar effect on any one of the components (see below) can be determined by entering incorrect data in the tabular formula and then substituting the correct data.

Sales revenue

Beginning inventory
+ Cost of goods purchased
= Cost of goods available for sale
– Ending inventory
= Cost of goods sold

– Cost of goods sold
= Gross profit

If the ending inventory of one period is incorrectly stated, it will affect the beginning inventory of the next period. The combined income for the two periods will be correct because the errors cancel each other out.

Balance Sheet Effects
Errors in inventory also affect the balance sheet. The effects can be determined by using the basic accounting equation: assets = liabilities + owner's equity. An understated ending inventory has no effect on liabilities, but will result in an understated owner's equity. An overstated ending inventory has no effect on liabilities, but will result in an overstated owner's equity.

Presentation and Analysis of Inventory

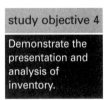

study objective 4

Demonstrate the presentation and analysis of inventory.

Inventory is usually the largest current asset on the balance sheet (ending inventory) and the largest expense on the income statement (cost of goods sold). Before reporting inventory on the financial statements, we must first ensure that it is properly valued.

Valuing Inventory at the Lower of Cost and Market (LCM)

The value of inventory items may fall because of changes in technology or style. When inventory values fall lower than cost, the inventory is written down to its market value. This is done by valuing the inventory at the lower of cost and market (LCM) in the period in which the decline occurs. This is in keeping with the conservative accounting practice, where the choice is the one that is least likely to overstate assets and net income.

The term "market" has recently been defined in Canada as net realizable value. Net realizable value is the selling price less any costs required to make the goods ready for sale. LCM is normally applied to each individual item rather than to total inventory. In some circumstances, similar or related items can be grouped together. LCM should be applied consistently from period to period.

Classifying and Reporting Inventory

Classification of inventory depends on whether the firm is a merchandiser or a manufacturer. A merchandiser buys its inventory, which is called merchandise inventory. Only one inventory category is recorded on the balance sheet. A manufacturer produces its inventory, which is classified into three categories depending on the state of completion: raw materials, work in process, and finished goods. Three inventory categories appear on the balance sheet of the manufacturer.

Inventory is classified as a current asset on the balance sheet. There should be disclosure of (1) major inventory classifications, (2) the basis of valuation (cost or lower of cost and market), and (3) the cost flow assumption being used (specific identification, FIFO, average cost, or LIFO). Disclosure is done in the notes to a company's financial statements.

Analysis

Inventories are important measures of business activity. Businesses must maintain a balance between too little inventory and too much inventory. Too much inventory is carried at a cost to the company; too little inventory would not be good for customer satisfaction. To measure the efficiency of inventory management, businesses use two ratios: the inventory turnover ratio and a related measure, the days sales in inventory.

Inventory Turnover
Inventory turnover is a liquidity ratio that measures the number of times, on average, inventory is sold during the period. It is calculated as follows:

Cost of Goods Sold ÷ Average Inventory = Inventory Turnover

The average inventory is used to ensure that the entire period is covered and is calculated using the average of the beginning and ending inventory balances. Inventory turnover is expressed in times (i.e., how many times inventory is turned over in an accounting period).

Days Sales in Inventory

This ratio converts the time of inventory turnover into days. It is calculated as follows:

Days in Year ÷ Inventory Turnover = Days Sales in Inventory

As with all ratios, the results of these measurements should be compared to the company's performance in prior years and to the industry average.

Appendix 6A

Inventory Cost Flow Assumptions in a Perpetual Inventory System

First-In, First-Out (FIFO)

The results of FIFO in a perpetual system are the same as in a periodic system. The cost of the oldest goods on hand prior to each sale is allocated to the cost of goods sold. The goods most recently purchased are allocated to the ending inventory.

Average Cost

Called the moving average cost in a perpetual system, it requires a new average to be calculated after each purchase. The average cost is then applied to (1) the units sold (cost of goods sold) and (2) the remaining units on hand (ending inventory). The dates of purchase and dates of sale become important in determining the moving average.

> **TIP**
> Each time the average cost is calculated, use the total cost of the inventory items on hand at the given date divided by the total units on hand at the same date.

study objective 5

Calculate ending inventory and cost of goods sold in a perpetual inventory system using inventory cost flow assumptions (Appendix 6A).

Last-In, First-Out (LIFO)

When a perpetual system is used, the cost of the most recent purchase prior to sale is allocated to the units sold as cost of goods sold. The earliest purchases remain on hand and are allocated to the ending inventory.

When we compare the cost of goods sold and ending inventory figures for all three perpetual cost flow assumptions, we know that FIFO gives the same results under both periodic and perpetual systems. The FIFO results differ from the average and LIFO, but the two assumptions are close in their proportionate outcomes.

Appendix 6B

Estimating Inventories

study objective 6

Estimate ending inventory using the gross profit and retail inventory methods (Appendix 6B).

There are times when it becomes necessary to estimate inventories. One such situation is when management wants to do monthly or quarterly financial statements and it is too costly to do an actual inventory count. Another situation might be when a fire or flood makes it impossible to take a physical inventory count. Inventory estimates are usually associated with the periodic system.

Two methods of estimating inventories are widely used: (1) the gross profit method and (2) the retail inventory method.

Gross Profit Method

The formulas for using the gross profit method are as follows:

Step 1

| Net Sales | – | Estimated Gross Profit (Net sales x gross profit margin) | = | Estimated Cost of Goods Sold |

Step 2

| Cost of Goods Available for Sale | – | Estimated Cost of Goods Sold | = | Estimated Cost of Ending Inventory |

Retail Inventory Method

The formulas for using the retail inventory method are as follows:

Step 1

| Cost of Goods Available for Sale at Retail | – | Net Sales | = | Ending Inventory at Retail |

Step 2

| Goods Available for Sale at Cost | ÷ | Goods Available for Sale at Retail | = | Cost-to-Retail Ratio |

Step 3

| Ending Inventory at Retail | x | Cost-to-Retail Ratio | = | Estimated Cost of Ending Inventory |

Demonstration Problem (SO 2)

Sanjay Company uses a periodic inventory system and had the following beginning inventory and purchases during 2008:

Date	Explanation	Units	Unit Cost	Total cost
Jan. 1	Inventory	400	$14	$ 5,600
Mar. 5	Purchase	200	15	3,000
May 15	Purchase	300	16	4,800
Oct. 4	Purchase	250	20	5,000
Dec. 16	Purchase	100	21	2,100
		1,250		$20,500

A physical count indicates that 550 units of inventory were on hand at December 31, 2008.

Instructions

Calculate the cost of goods sold and ending inventory under (a) FIFO, (b) average cost, and (c) LIFO.

Solution to Demonstration Problem

(a) FIFO:

Ending inventory:

Date	Units	Unit Cost	Total Cost
Dec. 16	100	$21	$2,100
Oct. 4	250	20	5,000
May 15	200	16	3,200
	550		$10,300

Cost of goods sold:

Cost of goods available for sale	$20,500
Less: Ending inventory	10,300
Cost of goods sold	$10,200

Proof of cost of goods sold:

Date	Units	Unit Cost	Total Cost
Jan. 1	400	$14	$5,600
Mar. 5	200	15	3,000
May 15	100	16	1,600
	700*		$10,200

*1,250 units available for sale – 550 in ending inventory = 700 units sold

(b) Average Cost:

Weighted-Average Unit Cost:

Cost of goods available for sale	÷	Total units available for sale	=	Weighted-average unit cost
$20,500	÷	1,250	=	$16.40

Ending Inventory:
  = $16.40 x 550 units = $9,020

Cost of good sold:

Cost of goods available for sale	$20,500
Less: Ending inventory	9,020
Cost of goods sold	$11,480

Proof of cost of goods sold:
  $16.40 x 700 units = $11,480

(c) LIFO:

Ending inventory:

Date	Units	Unit Cost	Total Cost
Jan. 1	400	$14	$5,600
Mar. 5	150	15	2,250
	550		$7,850

Cost of goods sold:

Cost of goods available for sale	$20,500
Less: Ending inventory	7,850
Cost of goods sold	$12,650

Proof of cost of goods sold:

Date	Units	Unit Cost	Total Cost
Dec. 16	100	$21	$ 2,100
Oct. 4	250	20	5,000
May 15	300	16	4,800
Mar. 5	50	15	750
	700		$12,650

Review Questions and Exercises

Multiple Choice

Circle the letter that best answers each of the following statements.

1. (SO 1) In determining ownership of goods for a seller, the cost of inventory must include which of the following?

   a. Consigned goods held at the seller's business place.
   b. Goods sold in transit, F.O.B. shipping point.
   c. Goods on hand for sale.
   d. Goods paid for by the buyer but still in the seller's possession.

2. (SO 1) The inventory for Marie's Company at December 31, 2008, was $300,000, based on a physical count of goods made on December 31. The following items were in transit:

   • Goods costing $5,000 were shipped F.O.B. destination on December 29, 2008, to a customer and received by the customer on January 3, 2009.

   • Goods costing $10,000 were shipped F.O.B. shipping point on December 30, 2008, to a customer and received by the customer on January 4, 2009.

   What amount should the company report as inventory on its December 31, 2008, balance sheet?

   a. $290,000
   b. $305,000
   c. $310,000
   d. $315,000

3. (SO 1) If beginning inventory is $80,000, cost of goods purchased is $420,000, and ending inventory is $75,000, what is the cost of goods sold?

   a. $420,000
   b. $415,000
   c. $425,000
   d. $500,000

4. (SO 2) The ideal method for allocating cost of goods available for sale to cost of goods sold and ending inventory, where the physical flow would exactly match the inventory valuation, would be:

a. first-in, first out.
b. last-in, first out.
c. specific identification.
d. average cost.

5. (SO 2) The cost flow assumption that will give the same result under both the perpetual and periodic inventory systems is the:

a. first-in, first out.
b. last-in, first out.
c. specific identification.
d. average cost.

6. (SO 3) The cost flow assumption that provides the best matching of current costs with current revenues is:

a. FIFO.
b. LIFO.
c. average cost.
d. specific identification.

7. (SO 4) The common practice used in valuing inventory at lower of cost and market is applying LCM to:

a. each individual item.
b. categories of items.
c. selected items.
d. total inventory.

8. (SO 2) Pocklington Company's periodic inventory records show the following data:

			Units	Cost
Inventory,	January	1	10,000	$9.00
Purchases:	June	18	9,000	8.00
	November	8	6,000	7.00

A physical inventory on December 31 shows 8,000 units on hand. Under the FIFO cost flow assumption, the December 31 inventory is:

a. $56,000.
b. $58,000.
c. $64,000.
d. $72,000.

9. (SO 4) Inventory items on an assembly line in various stages of production are classified as:

a. finished goods.
b. work in process.
c. raw materials.
d. merchandise inventory.

*10. (SO 5) The following data relates to Kent Company for the month of January:

		Units	Cost
Jan. 1	Beginning inventory	100	$10
Jan. 15	Purchase	200	13
Jan. 24	Sale	150	?
Jan. 29	Purchase	250	14

Under the average cost flow assumption, perpetual system, what is the cost of the inventory at January 31?

a. $5,000
b. $5,450
c. $5,300
d. $4,400

11. (SO 3) In a period of rising prices, FIFO will have a:

a. lower net income than LIFO.
b. lower cost of goods sold than LIFO.
c. lower ending inventory than LIFO.
d. lower net purchases than LIFO.

12. (SO 3) In a period of inflation, the use of LIFO will result in:

a. a more realistic inventory value than FIFO.
b. a better matching of costs and revenues than FIFO.
c. higher ending inventory than FIFO.
d. higher net income than FIFO.

13. (SO 3) On December 31, 2008, Kavin Company overstated its ending inventory by $4,000. Assuming no correcting entry was made, the effects on the 2009 income statement items are:

	Net Income	Sales	Cost of Goods Sold
a.	overstated	no effect	understated
b.	understated	no effect	overstated
c.	overstated	overstated	understated
d.	understated	no effect	understated

14. (SO 3) Newton's Company made an inventory count on December 31, 2008. During the count, one of the clerks made the error of counting an inventory item twice. For the balance sheet at December 31, 2008, the effects of this error are:

	Assets	Liabilities	Owner's Equity
a.	overstated	understated	overstated
b.	understated	no effect	understated
c.	overstated	no effect	overstated
d.	overstated	overstated	understated

15. (SO 4) On December 31, Hawk Company determined that inventory costing $18,000, with a sales price of $45,000, had a net realizable value of $16,000. What amount should be recorded for inventory on the balance sheet on December 31?

  a. $16,000
  b. $27,000
  c. $18,000
  d. $45,000

16. (SO 4) Kelly Company values its inventory on the balance sheet using the lower of cost and market rule. This is an application of:

  a. matching.
  b. double entry.
  c. conservatism.
  d. business entity.

Questions 17 and 18 are based on the following data:

Chris Bextor's Bookstore had 200 electric pencil sharpeners costing $18 each on hand at January 1. Purchases and sales of electric pencil sharpeners during the month of January were as follows:

Date	Purchases	Sales
Jan. 14		150 @ $28
17	100 @ $20	
25	100 @ $22	
29		100 @ $32

Chris Bextor maintains perpetual inventory records. According to a physical count, 150 electric pencil sharpeners were on hand at January 31.

*17.(SO 5) Under the FIFO cost flow assumption, what is the cost of the inventory at January 31?

  a. $400
  b. $3,060
  c. $3,100
  d. $3,200

*18.(SO 5) Under the average cost flow assumption, what is the cost of the inventory at January 31?

  a. $400
  b. $3,060
  c. $3,100
  d. $3,200

*19.(SO 5) Trans-Alta Company recorded the following data in its perpetual inventory system:

Date		Units	Inventory Balance	Unit Cost
Jan.1	Inventory		400	$1.00
Jan.8	Purchased	600	1,000	1.10
Jan.12	Sold	800	200	

What is the moving average cost per unit of the inventory at January 31?

a. $1.00
b. $1.05
c. $1.06
d. $1.10

*20.(SO 6) Doppler Company wishes to prepare an income statement for the month of March when its records show Net Sales, $300,000; Beginning Inventory, $59,000; and Cost of Goods Purchased, $155,000. The company realizes a 30 percent gross profit rate. What is the estimated cost of the ending inventory at March 31 under the gross profit method?

a. $4,000
b. $55,000
c. $63,000
d. $72,000

*21.(SO 6) Baker Company's records indicate the following information for the year:

Merchandise inventory, Jan.1	$ 550,000
Purchases	2,250,000
Net Sales	3,000,000

On December 31, a physical inventory determined that ending inventory of $600,000 was in the warehouse. Baker's gross profit on sales has remained constant at 30 percent. Baker suspects some of the inventory may have been taken by some new employees. At December 31, what is the estimated cost of missing inventory?

a. $100,000
b. $200,000
c. $300,000
d. $700,000

Questions 22 and 23 are based on the following data:

On December 31, Miller Retailers has the following information under the retail inventory method:

	Cost	Retail
Beginning inventory	$40,500	$ 57,000
Cost of goods purchased	57,000	73,000
Cost of goods available for sale	$97,500	130,000
Sales (net)		72,000
Ending inventory at retail		$ 58,000

*22.(SO 6) What is the cost-to-retail ratio?

a. 71%
b. 78%
c. 75%
d. 80%

*23.SO 6) What is the estimated cost of the ending inventory?

    a. $41,210
    b. $45,286
    c. $43,500
    d. $22,500

Matching

Match each term with its definition by writing the appropriate letter in the space provided.

Terms	Definitions
____ 1. Net realizable value	a. The number of times, on average, inventory is sold during the period.
____ 2. Days sales in inventory	b. The inventory costing method that tracks the actual physical flow of the goods available for sale.
____ 3. Specific identification	c. The inventory cost flow assumption that assumes that the latest units purchased are the first to be allocated to cost of goods sold.
____ 4. First-in, first-out (FIFO)	d. The inventory cost flow assumption that assumes that the earliest goods acquired are the first to be recognized as cost of goods sold.
____ 5. Average cost	e. The inventory cost flow assumption that assumes that it is impossible to measure a specific physical flow of inventory.
____ 6. Last-in, first-out (LIFO)	f. A method used to estimate the cost of the ending inventory by applying the gross profit margin to net sales.
____ 7. Retail inventory method	g. The selling price less any cost required to make the goods ready for sale.
____ 8. Gross profit method	h. The average number of days inventory is held.
____ 9. Lower of cost and market	i. A method for estimating the cost of the ending inventory by applying a cost-to-retail ratio.
____ 10. Inventory turnover	j. A basis for stating inventory at the lower of the original cost and net realizable value.

Exercises

E6-1   (SO 2 & 3) On January 1, Lady Jade Industries had beginning inventory of 500 units that cost $10 each. The following purchases and sales were made during the first six months of the year:

Date	Explanation	Units	Cost
Jan. 23	Sale	160	
Feb. 9	Purchase	300	$13
Mar. 15	Purchase	310	$12
Apr. 13	Sale	250	
May 26	Purchase	500	$11
June 4	Sale	200	
June 30	Sale	300	

Lady Jade Industries uses a periodic inventory system. On June 30, the count of the ending inventory was 700 units.

Instructions:
(a) Determine the cost of goods available for sale.

Cost of Goods Available for Sale

Date	Units	Unit Cost	Total Cost

(b) Determine the cost of the ending inventory and the cost of goods sold at June 30 for each of the following cost flow assumptions:

(1) FIFO

Ending Inventory:

Date	Units	Unit Cost	Total Cost

Cost of goods sold:

_____

_____

_____

_____

Proof of cost of goods sold:

Date	Units	Unit Cost	Total Cost

(2) Average cost

_____

_____

_____

_____

_____

(3) LIFO
Ending Inventory:

Date	Units	Unit Cost	Total Cost

Cost of goods sold:

_____

_____

_____

Proof of cost of goods sold:

Date	Units	Unit Cost	Total Cost

(c) Which cost flow assumption gives the highest ending inventory? Why?

_____

_____

_____

_____

(d) Which cost flow assumption results in the highest cost of goods sold? Why?

_____

_____

_____

_____

E6-2   (SO 3) Beagle Company reported the following income statement data for the years ended December 31:

BEAGLE COMPANY
Income Statement (partial)
December 31

	2008	2007
Sales	$395,000	$370,000
Cost of goods sold		
Beginning inventory	42,000	50,000
Cost of goods purchased	315,000	295,000
Cost of goods available for sale	357,000	345,000
Ending inventory	49,000	42,000
Cost of goods sold	308,000	303,000
Gross profit	$ 87,000	$ 67,000

The inventories at January 1, 2007, and December 31, 2008, are correct. However, the ending inventory at December 31, 2007, was understated by $15,000.

Instructions
(a) Prepare the correct income statement up to gross profit for the two years.

BEAGLE COMPANY
Income Statement (partial)
December 31

(b) What is the combined effect of the inventory error on total gross profit for the two years?

_____

_____

_____

*E6-3, *E6-4, and *E6-5 are based on the following data:

On January 1, Atco Industries had a beginning inventory of 200 units that cost $30 each. The following purchases and sales were made during the year:

Pool of Costs

Date	Explanation	Units	Cost
	Purchases and Sales		
Apr. 30	Sale	50	
May 5	Purchase	240	$28
June 10	Sale	180	
Aug. 8	Purchase	350	$31
Sept. 12	Sale	310	
Nov. 29	Purchase	300	$33
Dec. 1	Sale	50	

Atco Industries uses a perpetual inventory system. The count of the ending inventory was 500 units at December 31.

*E6-3   (SO 5) Calculate the cost of the ending inventory and the cost of goods sold for Atco Industries for the year ended December 31 using the first-in, first-out (FIFO) cost flow assumption.

FIFO:

Date	Purchases Units	Cost	Total	Cost of Goods Sold Units	Cost	Total	Balance Units	Cost	Total

*E6-4   (SO 5) Calculate the cost of the ending inventory and the cost of goods sold for Atco Industries for the year ended December 31 using the weighted-average cost flow assumption.

Weighted Average Cost:

	Purchases			Cost of Goods Sold			Balance		
Date	Units	Cost	Total	Units	Cost	Total	Units	Cost	Total

*E6-5   (SO 5) Calculate the cost of the ending inventory and the cost of goods sold for Atco Industries for the year ended December 31 using the last-in, first-out (LIFO) cost flow assumption.

LIFO:

Date	Purchases			Cost of Goods Sold			Balance		
	Units	Cost	Total	Units	Cost	Total	Units	Cost	Total

*E6-6   (SO 6) The records of the Bell Company show the following data for the month of October:

Net sales	$230,000
Inventory at cost, October 1	122,500
Inventory at retail, October 1	175,000
Goods purchased at cost	149,600
Goods purchased at retail	220,000

Instructions

(a) Using the retail inventory method, calculate the estimated cost of the inventory at October 31 (round to two decimals).

_____

_____

_____

_____

_____

_____

_____

(b) Assuming a gross profit margin of 30 percent, calculate the estimated cost of the inventory at October 31 using the gross profit method.

_____

_____

_____

_____

_____

_____

Solutions to Review Questions and Exercises

Multiple Choice

1. (c) Choice (c) is the only cost included in the cost of the inventory. The other costs belong to the consignor or to the buyer of the merchandise.

2. (b) The company should add the cost of the goods ($5,000) that are in transit with the terms F.O.B. destination. When goods are sent F.O.B. shipping point, ownership passes to the buyer when the carrier accepts the goods from the seller.

3. (c) Beginning inventory ($80,000) plus cost of goods purchased ($420,000) minus ending inventory ($75,000) equals cost of goods sold ($425,000).

4. (c) When possible, specific identification is the ideal method for allocating cost of goods available for sale.

5. (a) The FIFO cost flow assumption gives the same result under both the perpetual and periodic methods.

6. (b) LIFO provides the best income statement valuation. It matches current costs with current revenues. The most recently acquired goods are the most recent goods sold.

7. (a) LCM is usually applied item by item, rather than in total. In some circumstances, similar or related items can be grouped together.

8. (b) Under the FIFO cost flow assumption, the costs of the most recent purchases are assigned to the goods on hand as follows:

Date	Units		Unit Cost		Total Cost
Nov. 8	6,000	x	$7.00	=	$42,000
June 18	2,000	x	8.00	=	16,000
	8,000				$58,000

9. (b) Finished goods are completed and ready for sale, raw materials are inventory on hand waiting to be used in production, and merchandise inventory does not apply to a manufacturing company.

*10. (c) Under the average cost flow assumption, the weighted-average cost is determined and applied to the units sold as follows:

	Units		Unit Cost		Total Cost		
Beginning	100	x	$10.00	=	$1,000		
Purchase	200	x	13.00	=	2,600		
Weighted-average unit cost	300		÷		3,600	=	$12.00/unit
Sale	(150)	x	12.00	=	(1,800)		
Purchase	250	x	14.00	=	3,500		
Ending inventory	400				$5,300		

11. (b)   In a period of rising prices, FIFO will have a lower cost of goods sold than LIFO. This is because under FIFO, the earliest costs are assigned to cost of goods sold, whereas under LIFO, the latest costs are assigned to cost of goods sold. Net purchases will be the same under either assumption.

12. (b)   The use of the LIFO cost flow assumption will result in a better matching of costs and revenues. The use of the FIFO cost flow assumption will result in a more realistic inventory value (choice (a)). The use of the LIFO cost flow assumption will result in lower net income, not higher as choices (c) and (d) indicate.

13. (b)   The ending inventory on December 31, 2008, is the beginning inventory on January 1, 2009. When beginning inventory is overstated, cost of goods sold will be overstated and net income will be understated. The Sales account will not be affected.

14. (c)   By counting an inventory item twice, the ending inventory will be overstated. When ending inventory is overstated, net income is overstated and, therefore, owner's equity is overstated. The overstatement will have no effect on liabilities.

15. (a) $16,000—inventory is recorded at the lower of cost and market as measured by the net realizable value of the goods.

16. (c)   When the market value of inventory is lower than its cost, the inventory is written down to its net realizable value. This is an example of the accounting characteristic of conservatism.

*17. (d)   Under the FIFO cost flow assumption, the costs of the most recent purchases are assigned to the inventory as follows:

Date	Units		Cost		Total
Jan. 25	100	x	$22.00	=	$2,200
Jan. 17	50	x	20.00	=	1,000
	150				$3,200

*18. (b)   Under the average cost flow assumption, the cost of the 150 units remaining is $3,060 (150 units @ $20.40 per unit), calculated as follows:

Date	Purchases Units Cost Total	Cost of Goods Sold Units Cost Total	Balance Units Cost Total
Jan. 1			200 x $18.00 = $ 3,600
Jan. 14		150 x $18.00 = $2,700	50 x $18.00 = $ 900
Jan. 17	100 x $20 = $2,000		150 x $19.33 = $ 2,900
Jan. 25	100 x $22 = $2,200		250 x $20.40 = $ 5,100
Jan. 29		100 x $20.40 = $2,040	150 x $20.40 = $ 3,060

*19. (c) Average cost must be calculated at the end of the accounting period based on the weighted-average unit cost of goods available for sale during the period. The calculation is as follows:

Date	Units		Unit Cost		Total Cost
Jan. 1	400	x	$1.00	=	$ 400
Jan. 8	600	x	1.10	=	660
	1,000				$1,060

$1,060 ÷ 1,000 = $1.06

*20. (a) The estimated cost of ending inventory at March 31 under the gross profit method is as follows:

Net sales	$300,000
Less: Estimated gross profit ($30% x $300,000)	90,000
Estimated cost of goods sold	$210,000
Beginning inventory	$ 59,000
Cost of goods purchased	155,000
Cost of goods available for sale	214,000
Less: Estimated cost of goods sold	210,000
Estimated cost of ending inventory	$ 4,000

*21. (a) The estimated cost of ending inventory at December 31 under the gross profit method is as follows:

Net sales	$3,000,000
Less: Estimated gross profit (30% x $3,000,000)	900,000
Estimated cost of goods sold	$2,100,000
Beginning inventory	$ 550,000
Cost of goods purchased	2,250,000
Cost of goods available for sale	2,800,000
Less: Estimated cost of goods sold	2,100,000
Estimated cost of ending inventory	$ 700,000

Therefore the estimated cost of missing inventory is $100,000 ($700,000 – $600,000).

*22. (c) The cost-to-retail ratio is based on the cost of goods available for sale. The ratio is 75% ($97,500 ÷ $130,000).

*23. (c) The cost-to-retail ratio (75%) times the ending inventory at retail ($58,000) equals the ending inventory at cost ($43,500).

Matching

1.	g	5.	e	9.	j		
2.	h	6.	c	10.	a		
3.	b	7.	i				
4.	d	8.	f				

Exercises

E6-1

(a)

Cost of Goods Available for Sale

Date	Explanation	Units	Unit Cost	Total
Jan. 1	Beginning Inventory	500	$10	$ 5,000
Feb. 9	Purchase	300	13	3,900
Mar. 15	Purchase	310	12	3,720
May 26	Purchase	500	11	5,500
	Total	1,610		$ 18,120

(b)

(1) FIFO:

Ending Inventory

Date	Units	Cost	Total
May 26	500	$11	$5,500
Mar. 15	200	$12	2,400
	700		$7,900

Cost of Goods Sold: $18,120 – $7,900 = $10,220

Proof of Cost of Goods Sold

Date	Units	Cost	Total
Jan.1	500	$10	$ 5,000
Feb.9	300	$13	3,900
Mar.15	110	$12	1,320
	910*		$10,220

*1,610 units available for sale – 700 in ending inventory = 910 units sold

(2) Average Cost:

Weighted-average unit cost = $18,120 ÷ 1,610 units = $11.255 per unit

Ending inventory: 700 units x $11.255/unit = $7,878

Cost of goods sold: $18,120 – 7,878 = $10,242

Proof of cost of goods sold: 910 x $11.255 = $10,242

(3) LIFO:

Ending Inventory

Date	Units	Cost	Total
Jan. 1	500	$10	$5,000
Feb. 9	200	$13	2,600
	700		$7,600

Cost of Goods Sold: $18,120 − $7,600 = $10,520

Proof of Cost of Goods Sold

Date	Units	Cost	Total
May 26	500	$11	$ 5,500
Mar. 15	310	$12	3,720
Feb. 9	100	$13	1,300
	910		$10,520

(c) The FIFO method has produced the highest ending inventory because the cost of the last 500 units purchased is higher than the 500 units on hand at the beginning of the year. With FIFO, the earliest costs are assigned to cost of goods sold, and the latest costs remain in ending inventory. For Lady Jade Industries, the ending inventory under FIFO is $7,900, compared to $7,878 under the weighted average method, and $7,600 under the LIFO method. FIFO will always have the highest ending inventory when prices are rising. In this situation prices rose and then started falling. When this happens FIFO will not necessarily have the highest ending inventory.

(d) The LIFO method has produced the highest cost of goods sold for Lady Jade Industries. Under LIFO, the most recent costs are charged to cost of goods sold, and the earliest costs are included in the ending inventory. The cost of goods sold under LIFO is $10,520, compared to $10,242 under the weighted-average method, and $10,220 under the FIFO method. FIFO will always have the highest ending inventory when prices are rising. In this situation prices rose and then started falling. When this happens FIFO will not necessarily have the highest ending inventory.

E6-2
(a)

BEAGLE COMPANY
Income Statement (partial)
December 31

	2008	2007
Sales	$395,000*	$370,000
Cost of goods sold		
Beginning inventory	57,000	50,000
Cost of goods purchased	315,000	295,000
Cost of goods available for sale	372,000	345,000
Ending inventory	49,000	57,000*
Cost of goods sold	323,000	288,000
Gross profit	$ 72,000	$ 82,000

* $42,000 + $15,000 = $57,000

(b) The cumulative effect on total gross profit for the two years is zero, as shown below:

Incorrect gross profits:	$87,000 + $67,000	= $154,000
Correct gross profits:	$72,000 + $82,000	= 154,000
Difference		$ 0

*E6-3
FIFO:

Date	Purchases Units Cost Total	Cost of Goods Sold Units Cost Total	Balance Units Cost Total
Jan. 1			200 x $30 = $ 6,000
Apr. 30		50 x 30 = $1,500	150 x 30 = $ 4,500
May 5	240 x 28 = $ 6,720		(150 x 30 240 x 28)= $11,220
Jun. 10		(150 x 30 30 x 28) = $5,340	210 x 28 = $ 5,880
Aug. 8	350 x 31 = $10,850		(210 x 28 350 x 31)= $16,730
Sept.12		(210 x 28 100 x 31)= $8,980	250 x 31 = $ 7,750
Nov. 29	300 x 33 = $ 9,900		(250 x 31 300 x 33)= $17,650
Dec. 1		50 x 31 = $1,550	(200 x 31 300 x 33)= $16,100
		$17,370	

*E6-4
Average Cost

Date	Purchases Units Cost Total	Cost of Goods Sold Units Cost Total	Balance Units Cost Total
Jan. 1			200 x $30.00 = $ 6,000
Apr. 30		50 x $30.00 = $1,500	150 x $30.00 = $ 4,500
May 5	240 x $28 = $ 6,720		390 x $28.77 = $11,220
Jun. 10		180 x $28.77 = $5,179	210 x $28.77 = $ 6,041
Aug. 8	350 x $31 = $10,850		560 x $30.16 = $16,891
Sept.12		310 x $30.16 = $9,350	250 x $30.16 = $ 7,540
Nov. 29	300 x $33 = $ 9,900		550 x $31.71 = $17,440
Dec. 1		50 x $31.71 = $1,586	500 x $31.71 = $15,855
		$17,615	

*E6-5
LIFO:

Date	Purchases Units Cost Total	Cost of Goods Sold Units Cost Total	Balance Units Cost Total
Jan 1			200 x $30 = $6,000
Apr. 30		50 x $30 = $1,500	150 x $30 = $4,500
May 5	240 x $28 = $6,720		(150 x $30
			240 x $28) = $11,220
Jun. 10		180 x $28 = $5,040	(150 x $30
			60 x $28) = $6,180
Aug. 8	350 x $31 =$10,850		(150 x $30
			60 x $28
			350 x $31) = $17,030
Sept.12		310 x $31 = $9,610	(150 x $30
			60 x $28
			40 x $31) = $ 7,420
Nov. 29	300 x $33 =$ 9,900		(150 x $30
			60 x $28
			40 x $31
			300 x $33) = $17,320
Dec. 1		50 x $33 = $1,650	(150 x $30
			60 x $28
			40 x $31
		$17,800	250 x $33) = $15,670

*E6-6

(a)

	Cost	Retail
Beginning inventory	$122,500	$175,000
Goods purchased	149,600	220,000
Goods available for sale	$272,100	395,000
Net sales		230,000
(1) Ending inventory at retail		$165,000

(2) Cost-to-retail ratio = ($272,100 ÷ $395,000) = 68.89%

(3) Ending inventory at cost = ($165,000 x 68.89%) = $113,668.50

(b)

Net sales	$230,000
Less: Estimated gross profit (30% x $230,000)	69,000
Estimated cost of goods sold	$161,000
Beginning inventory	$122,500
Cost of goods purchased	149,600
Cost of goods available for sale	272,100
Less: Estimated cost of goods sold	161,000
Estimated cost of ending inventory	$111,100

chapter 7

Internal Control and Cash

study objectives >>

After studying this chapter, you should be able to:
1. Explain the activities that help achieve internal control.
2. Apply control activities to cash receipts.
3. Apply control activities to cash disbursements.
4. Operate and account for a petty cash fund.
5. Describe the control features of a bank account.
6. Prepare a bank reconciliation.
7. Report cash on the balance sheet.

Preview of Chapter 7

This chapter explains the important features of an internal control system and how those controls apply to cash receipts and disbursements, including the use of a petty cash fund. The use of a bank account and how cash is reported on the balance sheet is also explained. The chapter is organized as follows:

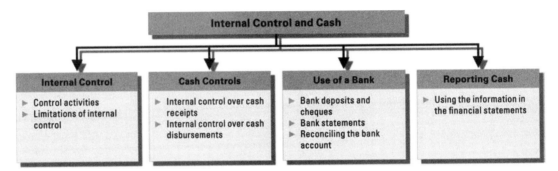

Internal Control

study objective 1

Explain the activities that help achieve internal control.

Internal control is the process that management designs and implements to help an organization achieve:
1. reliable financial reporting,
2. effective and efficient operations,
3. compliance with relevant laws and regulations.

The accounting system—the procedures and records created to record, process, and report the organization's transactions—is part of an internal control system.

Control Activities

Control activities are the policies and procedures that help ensure that management's directions are followed. Specific actions must be taken in response to risks that threaten the achievement of reliable financial reporting, effective and efficient operations, and compliance with relevant laws and regulations. They are as follows:
1. Establishment of responsibility
2. Segregation of duties
3. Documentation procedures
4. Physical controls
5. Performance reviews
6. Other controls

The specific control activities that are used in any company depend on the size and type of business and on management's control philosophy.

Establishment of Responsibility
An essential control activity is the assignment of responsibility to specific individuals. Control is most effective when only one person is responsible for a given task. If only one person has operated the cash register at the grocery store, that person will be responsible for any cash shortages. If two or more persons have worked the register, it may be impossible to determine who is responsible for any errors that might have occurred.

Segregation of Duties

Segregation of duties refers to the division of related tasks to involve more than one employee. Related activities should never be assigned to only one person, since it increases the potential for errors and irregularities.

In addition, the accounting for an asset (record keeping) should be separate from the physical custody of that asset. For example, if a receptionist is responsible for opening the mail and sorting the cheques received from customers for payment on account (physical custody), an accounting assistant should be responsible for preparing the bank deposit record (record keeping).

Documentation Procedures

Documentation procedures provide evidence that transactions and events have happened. Common examples of documentation include pre-numbered sales invoices, cheques, purchase orders, and so on. All pre-numbered documents must be accounted for. Adding signatures or initials to documents also helps to identify the individual(s) responsible for the transaction or event.

Physical Controls

Physical controls include mechanical and electronic controls used to safeguard (protect) assets. These controls include safes, vaults, and safety deposit boxes for the storage of cash and important business papers; alarms to prevent break-ins; television monitors and garment sensors to deter theft; and locked warehouses to house inventory.

Computer systems that are password protected are equipped with program controls built-in to prevent intentional and unintentional errors and unauthorized access.

Performance Reviews

Most control systems include independent internal and/or external reviews of performance and records. Performance and data are reviewed, compared, and reconciled by one or several employees. Reviews are done periodically or on a surprise basis and should be done by a person independent of the employee who is being reviewed. Discrepancies recognized should be reported to management so that the situation can be corrected.

Internal Review: In large companies, independent internal verification is often assigned to internal auditors. Internal auditors are employees of the company who evaluate the effectiveness of the company's system of internal control. They periodically review the activities of departments and individuals to determine whether the correct control activities are being followed.

External Review: External auditors are independent of the company. They are professional accountants hired by the company to confirm the fair presentation of the company's financial statements. While they need to understand a company's internal controls, they are not required to test how effective the controls are or to give any kind of assurance about a company's internal control system. In Canada, it is management's responsibility to evaluate the internal control systems.

Other Controls

Other control measures can include:
1. Bonding employees who handle cash, which means getting insurance protection against theft of assets by dishonest employees.
2. Rotating employees' duties and requiring employees to take vacations. This discourages employees from attempting theft, since they will not be able to hide their improper actions.

Limitations of Internal Control

Regardless of how an internal control system is designed, it can only give reasonable assurance that assets are properly safeguarded and that the accounting records are reliable. The concept of reasonable assurance rests on the premise that the costs of establishing control procedures should not exceed their expected benefits.

The human factor is also an important limit in every system of internal control. A good system can become ineffective through employee fatigue, carelessness, or indifference. Collusion results when two or more individuals work together to get around prescribed controls and eliminates the effectiveness of a system. In a computerized system, breakdowns in internal control can occur because of human errors.

Cash Controls

Cash is easily concealed and transported and lacks owner identification, making it very susceptible to theft. To safeguard cash and to assure the accuracy of the accounting records for cash, effective internal control over cash is highly desirable.

Internal Control over Cash Receipts

study objective 2

Apply control activities to cash receipts.

Cash receipts come from cash sales, collection on accounts from customers, the receipt of interest, dividends, rents, investments by owners, bank loans, and proceeds from sales of property, plant, and equipment. It is important to have good controls in place to safeguard these receipts.

To show how internal control is applied, we will examine control activities for a retail store with reference to over-the-counter, mail-in, and electronic receipts.

Over-the-Counter Receipts

Control of over-the-counter receipts is centred on cash registers that are visible to customers. When a sale is rung up, the amount of the sale should be clearly visible to the customer. This prevents the cashier from entering a lower amount and keeping the extra cash. The customer receives an itemized receipt and, if paying with cash, is expected to count the change received.

Most customers pay with a debit or credit card. Debit cards give customers access to the money in their own bank accounts. Credit cards give customers access to money made available by a bank or other financial institution. Cards are convenient for customers and improve internal controls for businesses because employees handle less cash.

Most companies track the type of payment through point-of-sale cash registers; daily sales are separated by type—cash, debit card, credit card, or cheque. Cash registers show each transaction, totals for each type of receipt, and an overall total.

At the end of a cashier's shift, the cashier counts the cash in the register and records the amount. This record is turned over to a supervisor or some other responsible employee to be verified and deposited in the bank. All cash receipts should be deposited daily, intact, into the bank account. An independent person who does not handle the cash should make sure that the amount deposited at the bank agrees with the cash register tapes and the accounting records. These are important control functions.

Debit Card Transactions:
Sales using debit cards are considered cash transactions. When a debit card sale occurs, the bank immediately deducts the cost of the purchase from the customer's bank account. The retailer can choose to have the amounts deposited in the retailer's

bank account daily or at some other convenient time. Banks charge the retailer a transaction fee for each debit card transaction.

For example, assume that on July 20, a retailer makes 15 debit card sales that total $350. The bank charges a fee of $0.40 per transaction and the total is transferred to the retailer's account on a daily basis. The entry to record the transaction is as follows:

Jul. 20	Cash	344	
	Debit Card Expense (15 x $0.40)	6	
	Sales		350
	To record debit card sales		

Credit Card Transactions: Sales using credit cards issued by banks, such as Visa and MasterCard, are considered cash sales by the retailer. Customers have access to money made available by a bank or other financial institution. In fact, the amount is loaned to the credit card user.

When a customer uses a credit card, the bank transfers the amount of the sale to the retailer, less a service fee. The fee for credit transactions is usually higher than debit card fees. The sale and the journal entry are similar to the debit card sale. Sales using the retailer's own credit card are credit sales and result in an accounts receivable, not cash at point of sale.

Mail-In Receipts

Cheques received through the mail are mail-in receipts. All mail should be opened by two mail clerks and should be promptly stamped "For Deposit Only," which will restrict the deposit of the cheque to any other person or business.

A daily list of cheques with details should be prepared in duplicate and signed by the mail clerks. The original list should be sent to the cashier's department, and the duplicate copy is sent to the accounting department. The list sent to the accounting department will be recorded as a journal entry to debit Cash and credit Accounts Receivable or Sales as required. The accounting department compares the list to the copy of the bank deposits to make sure that all mail-in receipts were included in the bank deposit.

Electronic Receipts

Electronic funds transfer (EFT) systems transfer funds between parties without the use of paper documents. Electronic receipts occur when amounts are transferred from a customer's bank account to the retailer's bank account. Using on-line banking to pay bills is another type of EFT transaction. On-line banking involves the use of the Internet as a means to transfer funds between bank accounts.

Debit and credit card transactions are also examples of electronic funds transfers. In Canada, the increased use of debit cards, credit cards, on-line banking, telephone banking, automated banking machines (ABMs), and pre-authorized payments have resulted in a decline in customer payments by cheque. This has resulted in better internal control over cash, since little or no cash is handled by company employees.

Internal Control over Cash Disbursements

Generally, internal control over cash disbursements is more effective when payments are made by cheque or EFT rather than by cash, except for incidental amounts, which are paid out of petty cash.

study objective 3

Apply control activities to cash disbursements.

Cheques

Internal controls over cheques include the signing of cheques by an authorized person or persons (cheques often require two signatures). Segregation of duties requires that the signing function be separate from the accounts payable function.

Cheques should be pre-numbered, and all cheques must be accounted for in the payment and recording process. Cheques should never be pre-signed, and blank cheques should be guarded.

When goods are received, a receiving report is matched to a purchase order. Authorized purchase orders, prepared by the purchasing department, are used to control expenditures and cash disbursements.

Electronic Payments

Many companies make payments to suppliers and employees using electronic funds transfer systems. An employee's salary may be paid using a direct deposit option. Cash is transferred from the company's bank account to the employee's bank account with no cheques being issued.

Pre-authorized payments of loans and other recurring payments are often made electronically as well. Persons independent of the accounts payable department should check that the payments agree with a list of authorized electronic payments.

Petty Cash Fund

study objective 4

Operate and account for a petty cash fund.

A petty cash fund is used to pay relatively small amounts. It contains a small amount of the company's cash that is physically kept at the company's place of business.

The petty cash fund is operated on an imprest system—money advanced for a specific purpose. Accounting for petty cash involves (1) establishing the fund, (2) making payments from the fund, and (3) replenishing the fund.

Establishing the Fund: Establishing a petty cash fund requires two steps: (1) appoint a petty cash custodian and (2) determine the size of the fund. A company cheque made payable to the petty cash custodian is issued.

The petty cash custodian keeps the cash in a locked box or drawer and is the only person authorized to make payments from the fund. The only time the Petty Cash account is used is when the fund is increased or decreased.

Making Payments from the Fund: The custodian of the petty cash fund has the authority to make payments from the fund in accordance with management policies. Each payment from the fund should be documented on a pre-numbered petty cash receipt and signed by both the custodian and the person who receives payment.

No accounting entry is required when payments are made from the fund. The sum of the petty cash receipts and money in the fund should be equal to the established total of the petty cash fund at all times. Surprise counts by an independent person should be made at any time to ensure that the fund is being properly used.

Replenishing the Fund: The petty cash fund should be replenished when the cash in the fund reaches a minimum level. The receipts, kept in the cash box, are examined to verify proper payment and summarized to recognize the expenses incurred through petty cash payments. When a cheque is issued to replenish the fund, then all the expenses are recorded as debits with a credit to Cash. The Petty Cash account is not affected when the fund is replenished.

Sometimes cash receipts plus cash in the petty cash box do not equal the total amount of the established petty cash fund. If the total amount is over or short of the established amount, an account called Cash Over or Short is used to record the difference. Cash over is recorded as a credit, and cash short is recorded as a debit to the account. Cash Over or Short is reported on the income statement.

If the Petty Cash account is not large enough, it is often increased when the fund is replenished. The account Petty Cash is debited to record the increase. If the account is too large, the account Petty Cash is credited to record the decrease. A petty cash fund must be replenished at the end of the accounting period regardless of how much cash is in the fund. This is done to recognize the effect of petty cash payments on the financial statements.

Use of a Bank

Using a bank makes internal control over cash much stronger. It creates a double record of all bank transactions—one by the business and the other by the bank. A company reduces the amount of currency that is kept on hand by depositing its cash at a bank.

study objective 5

Describe the control features of a bank account.

Bank Deposits and Cheques

Bank deposits should be made by an authorized employee and documented by a deposit slip. Deposits made by direct deposit, through automated bank machines (ABMs), or electronic funds transfers (EFT) are found on bank statements.

A cheque is a written order signed by the depositor directing the bank to pay a specified sum of money to a designated recipient. The three parties to a cheque are as follows: (1) the maker (or drawer) who issues the cheque, (2) the bank (or payer) on which the cheque is drawn, and (3) the payee to whom the cheque is payable.

Clearing occurs when a cheque or deposit is accepted by the maker's bank. The clearing process involves the actual flow of cash through the banking system. Money flows from one financial institution to another when a payee presents the maker's cheque at a bank and the cheque is sent back to the maker's bank.

The clearing process for electronic payments is more direct than for cheques and other paper-based items. There is no requirement to deliver a physical payment item in these cases.

Bank Statements

A bank statement shows the depositor's bank transactions and balance. A typical statement shows the following:
1. cheques paid and other debits that reduce the balance in the depositor's account,
2. deposits and other credits that increase the balance in the depositor's account, and
3. the account balance after each day's transactions.

It would appear that the debits and credits reported on the bank statement are backwards, but this isn't really true. The cash in your bank account is a liability account at the bank. It must be repaid to you when you request it. Liabilities are increased by credits and decreased by debits.

Debit memorandum
Banks charge fees for using their services. A debit memorandum (DM) is usually included with the bank statement to explain charges against the depositor's account such as bank service charges, the cost of printing cheques, certifying cheques, issuing traveller's cheques, transferring funds to other locations, and cheques marked NSF (not sufficient funds).

Credit memorandum

A credit memorandum (CM) shows items such as interest earned by the depositor on funds on deposit. It may also represent funds electronically transferred into the depositor's account and any other amounts added to the depositor's account.

Reconciling the Bank Account

The bank and the depositor keep independent records of the depositor's account. As it happens, the two balances are almost never the same at any specific time. The process of making the book balance agree with the bank balance is called reconciling the bank account.

The lack of agreement may be the result of time lags, where one party does not record a transaction in the same period as the other, or errors by either party in recording transactions. Except in electronic banking applications, time lags often happen.

Reconciliation Procedure

study objective 6

Prepare a bank reconciliation.

The bank reconciliation should be prepared by an employee who has no direct responsibilities relating to cash or by the owner of the company.

The reconciling procedure involves reconciling the balance per books and balance per bank to their adjusted cash balances. The adjusted cash balances should be exactly equal.

The following items are taken into account when determining the adjusted cash balance per the bank:
1. Determine deposits in transit.
2. Determine outstanding cheques.
3. Determine any bank errors.

The following items are taken into account when determining the adjusted cash balance per the company's books:
1. Include credit memoranda.
2. Include debit memoranda.
3. Determine any company errors.

The following table summarizes the reconciling items required to make the bank's records and the depositor's books balance.

Adjustment to Bank	Adjustment to Depositor's Books
Deposits in transit have been recorded in the books of the depositor, but have not been recorded by the bank.	
Outstanding cheques have been recorded in the books of and issued by the depositor, but have not yet been paid by the bank.	
Errors made by the bank must be an adjustment to the bank.	**Errors** made by the depositor must be an adjustment to the books.
	Bank memoranda could be deductions (DM) or additions (CM) to the depositor's books.

Each reconciling item used in determining the adjusted cash balance per books should be recorded in the depositor's books as an adjustment to the Cash account through general journal entries. The adjusting entries will be shown in the Demonstration Problem at the end of this chapter.

Reporting Cash

Cash consists of coins, currency (paper money), cheques, money orders, and money on hand or on deposit in a bank or similar depository. Debit card transactions and bank credit card slips are cash, but non-bank credit card slips are not.

study objective 7

Report cash on the balance sheet.

Cash on hand, cash in banks, and petty cash are normally combined and reported as Cash on the balance sheet. Because cash is the most liquid asset owned by a company, it is listed first in the current asset section of the balance sheet.

Cash equivalents are short-term, highly liquid (easily sold) investments. They include short-term deposits, treasury bills, and money markets funds. Cash equivalents generally have maturities of three months or less. Many companies combine cash and cash equivalents on the balance sheet.

A cash deficit occurs when a company's bank account is in a negative position. The Cash account in the general ledger would show a credit balance. It is, in fact, a short-term loan from the bank (overdraft at the bank) and should be reported as a current liability called **bank indebtedness** (loan) on the balance sheet.

A company may have cash that is not available for general use because it is restricted for a special purpose. Significant amounts of cash for restricted use should be reported separately on the balance sheet as restricted cash in the current asset section if it will be used in the next year. If it is to be held for a longer time, it should be reported as a non-current asset.

Using the Information in the Financial Statements

Cash management requires that enough cash is on hand to pay bills as they come due. But too much cash on hand may indicate that management is not maximizing its return on assets. Two useful pieces of information that help assess management's effectiveness in controlling cash are (1) the cash flow statement and (2) the management report.

The cash flow statement provides information as to where cash came from and what it was used for. The management report includes acknowledgement of management's responsibility for the development of internal controls over the financial reporting process.

Demonstration Problem (SO 6)

The information below relates to the Cash account in the ledger of Mozart Corporation for November 2008:

Balance November 1	$27,100
Add: November deposits	94,500
Less: November cheques written	(93,400)
Balance November 30	$28,200

MOZART CORPORATION
Bank Statement
November 30, 2008

	Cheques and Other Debits	Deposits and Other Credits	Balance
Balance, November 1			20,300
November deposits		90,500	
Cheques cleared in November	88,000		
EFT from customer		5,000	
NSF cheques ($415 + $10 service charge)	425		
Service charge	25		
Interest on loan	125		
			27,225

Additional information:
1. There was a deposit of $6,800 in transit at October 31, which cleared the bank in November.
2. There were no outstanding cheques at November 1.
3. The EFT payment from L. Borrings, a customer, was received during November.
4. The NSF cheque was for $415 from L. Katura, a customer, in payment of her account. The bank added a $10 processing fee.

Instructions
(a) Prepare the bank reconciliation at November 30, 2008.
(b) Journalize the entries required by the reconciliation.

Solution to Demonstration Problem

(a)

MOZART CORPORATION
Bank Reconciliation
November 30, 2008

Cash balance per bank statement		$27,225
Add: Deposits in transit ($94,500 + $6,800 – $90,500)		10,800
		38,025
Less: Outstanding cheques ($93,400 – $88,000)		5,400
Adjusted cash balance per bank		$32,625
Cash balance per books		$28,200
Add: EFT transfer from customer		5,000
		33,200
Less: NSF cheques ($415 + $10)	$425	
Bank service charge	25	
Interest on loan	125	575
Adjusted cash balance per books		$32,625

(b)

Nov.	30	Interest Expense	125	
		Cash		125
		To record interest paid on loan		

	30	Bank Charges Expense	25	
		Cash		25
		To record bank service charges.		

	30	Accounts Receivable	425	
		Cash		425
		To re-establish accounts receivable for		
		L. Katura, NSF cheques, and processing fee		

	30	Cash	5,000	
		Accounts Receivable		5,000
		EFT receipt from L Borrings, customer		

Review Questions and Exercises

Multiple Choice

Circle the letter that best answers each of the following statements.

1. (SO 1) Internal control is the process that management designs and implements to help an organization achieve:

    a. compliance with relevant laws and regulations.
    b. effective and efficient operations.
    c. reliable financial reporting.
    d. all of the above.

2. (SO 1) Which of the following is an example of poor internal control?

    a. The accountant does not have physical custody of the asset or access to it.
    b. The custodian of an asset maintains the asset, but does not have access to the accounting records.
    c. One person is given the responsibility for handling related transactions.
    d. A salesperson makes the sale, and a different person ships the goods.

3. (SO 1) Independent internal reviews of performance or records are not involved when an independent person:

    a. reconciles the cash balance per books with the cash balance per the bank.
    b. reviews the accounts receivable subsidiary ledger.
    c. makes a surprise count of the petty cash fund.
    d. is responsible for making sales and recording the entries in the books.

4. (SO 1) Internal auditors:

	are employees of the company	review activities of departments for compliance with prescribed internal controls
a.	yes	yes
b.	yes	no
c.	no	yes
d.	no	no

5. (SO 1) Which of the following is not a physical control?

  a. Alarms
  b. Bonding of employees
  c. Safety deposit boxes
  d. Fences around storage areas

6. (SO 1) Which of the following is not an example of an effective internal control measure?

  a. Requiring employees to take vacations
  b. Pre-numbering sales invoices
  c. Bonding employees who handle cash
  d. Permitting collusion among employees

7. (SO 1) Which of the following statements concerning the limitations of internal control is correct?

  a. The human factor is unimportant.
  b. The costs of establishing control procedures should not exceed their expected benefits.
  c. Collusion among employees may result in more effective control.
  d. A system of internal control should be infallible.

8. (SO 2) Cash receipt transactions are not effectively controlled when:

  a. cash registers are used in executing cash receipt transactions.
  b. personnel who handle cash receipts are bonded.
  c. the company's safes and vaults are used for the storage of cash before it is deposited.
  d. one individual is responsible for the receiving, recording, and custody of cash receipts.

9. (SO 2) Independent review of performance and records over cash receipt transactions does not occur when:

  a. cashiers count cash daily and compare the total to cash register totals.
  b. the treasurer's office makes daily comparisons of total receipts and receipts deposited in the bank.
  c. an internal auditor reconciles bank and book balances monthly.
  d. cash receipts are deposited in the bank daily after being checked by the supervisor.

10. (SO 2) Storing cash in a company safe is an application of which internal control activity?

    a. Segregation of duties
    b. Documentation procedures
    c. Physical controls
    d. Establishment of responsibility

11. (SO 2) Which of the following statements is true about debit card transactions?

    a. Debit cards give customers access to money made available by their bank.
    b. The retailer is charged a transaction fee for each debit card transaction.
    c. The fee for the bank debit card is usually higher than the fee for the bank credit card.
    d. With debit cards, banks take a risk on the customer's creditworthiness.

12. (SO 2) Electronic funds transfers result in better internal control for all of the following reasons except:

    a. the cash is instantly transferred from the customer to the company's bank.
    b. no cash or cheques are handled by company employees.
    c. there is evidence of the transfer on the bank statement.
    d. the credit memorandum might not be in agreement with the transfer amount.

13. (SO 3) Which of the following statements about internal control over cash disbursements is incorrect?

    a. More effective internal control results when payments are made by cheque rather than in cash.
    b. The bank reconciliation should be prepared by the employee who writes the cheques.
    c. The use of a bank contributes significantly to good internal control over cash disbursements.
    d. Pre-numbered cheques should be used and all cheques in a series should be accounted for.

14. (SO 3) Which of the following is an application of good internal control over cash disbursements?

    a. Upon payment, the approved invoice should be stamped PAID.
    b. Blank cheques should be stored in the treasurer's desk.
    c. Each cheque should be compared with the approved invoice after the cheque is issued.
    d. Cheque signers should record the cash disbursements.

15. (SO 3) Which of the following statements is untrue about electronic payments?

    a. Direct deposit of salaries paid to employees is an electronic payment.
    b. Electronic payments of accounts payable cannot be made by companies; they must use cheques.
    c. EFT payments reduce company costs.
    d. Pre-authorized payments are referenced on the bank statement with the name of the company paid.

16. (SO 4) When making a payment from the petty cash fund for postage stamps, the following journal entry is made.

   a. Office Supplies   XXXX
         Petty Cash   XXXX
   b. Postage Expense   XXXX
         Petty Cash   XXXX
   c. Miscellaneous Expense   XXXX
         Petty Cash   XXXX
   d. No entry is made.

17. (SO 4) A $100 petty cash fund contains $92 in receipts and $7 in cash. The entry to record replenishments of the fund will include a debit to:

   a. Petty Cash for $100.
   b. Cash Over and Short for $1.
   c. Expenses for $93.
   d. Petty Cash for $8.

18. (SO 4) Which of the following statements is true about the petty cash fund?

   a. The custodian and one other person are authorized to make payments from the fund.
   b. Any size of expenditure can be made from the fund.
   c. When a payment is made from the fund, only the person who has custody of the fund is required to sign the petty cash receipt.
   d. No accounting entry is made at the time of payment from the fund since it is unnecessary and inefficient to do so.

19. (SO 4) Which of the following statements is false about the petty cash fund?

   a. Receipts and supporting documents are examined before the fund is replenished to verify proper payments have been made from the fund.
   b. The petty cash fund is replenished at the end of the accounting period regardless of how much cash is in the fund.
   c. When the fund is replenished, the total amount of the receipts is the amount of the cheque made to replenish the fund.
   d. Internal control of the petty cash fund is strengthened by cancelling the paid receipts so they cannot be resubmitted for reimbursement.

20. (SO 5) Which of the following statements is false?

   a. The use of a bank contributes significantly to good internal control over cash.
   b. Many companies have only one bank account.
   c. Use of a bank minimizes the amount of currency that must be kept on hand.
   d. A company can safeguard its cash by using a bank as a depository and a clearing house for cheques received and cheques written.

21. (SO 5) The person who issues the cheque is known as the:

   a. maker.
   b. payer.
   c. payee.
   d. drawee.

22. (SO 5) Which of the following statements is false about bank transactions?

    a. Deposits may be made by any company employee available to do so.
    b. ABM cash withdrawals are not allowed on a business bank account where two signatures are required on cheques.
    c. It is important to know the balance of the chequing account at all times, whether a computerized or manual accounting system is used by the business.
    d. Clearing happens when a cheque or deposit is accepted by the maker's bank.

23. (SO 6) A bank statement will show a credit entry for:

    a. a bank service charge.
    b. an NSF (not sufficient funds) cheque from a customer.
    c. an EFT transfer made to the depositor's account.
    d. the cost of printing cheques.

24. (SO 6) Which of the following reconciling items would be added to the balance per bank statement to determine the adjusted balance per bank?

	Deposits in Transit	Outstanding Cheques	NSF Cheques
a.	yes	yes	yes
b.	no	yes	no
c.	yes	no	no
d.	yes	yes	no

25. (SO 6) Which of the following statements about a bank reconciliation is incorrect?

    a. It is an unnecessary process since the bank's records and the depositor's records are in agreement at the end of the period.
    b. It is done because deposits in transit are not included in the bank's balance.
    c. It is done because outstanding cheques are included in the book balance but not in the bank balance.
    d. Credit memoranda are included in the bank's balance but not in the book's balance.

26. (SO 7) Which of the following is not considered cash?

    a. Money orders
    b. Postdated cheques
    c. Bank deposits
    d. Currency

27. (SO 7) Cash equivalents are highly liquid investments that can be converted into a specific amount of cash. They typically have maturities of:

    a. one month or less when purchased.
    b. three months or less when purchased.
    c. six months or less when purchased.
    d. one year or less when purchased.

28. (SO 7) Which of the following statements about the presentation of cash on the balance sheet is incorrect?

   a. Restricted cash balances should be reported separately.
   b. If the Cash account has a credit balance, it should be reported as a current liability.
   c. Cash is reported first on the balance sheet because it is the most liquid asset owned by the company.
   d. Petty cash must be reported separately from Cash.

Matching

Match each term with its definition by writing the appropriate letter in the space provided.

Terms

_____ 1. Internal control

_____ 2. Cash

_____ 3. Bank overdraft

_____ 4. Internal auditors

_____ 5. Outstanding cheques

_____ 6. Deposits in transit

_____ 7. Bank statement

_____ 8. Petty cash fund

_____ 9. Electronic funds transfer

Definitions

a. Resources, such as coins, currency, cheques, or money orders, that are accepted at face value in a bank or similar depository.

b. Company employees who evaluate the effectiveness of the company's internal control system on a continuous basis.

c. A cash fund used to pay small amounts.

d. An excess of withdrawals over the amount available in the depositor's bank account.

e. The processes designed and implemented by management that help an organization to achieve reliable financial reporting, effective and efficient operations, and compliance with relevant laws and regulations.

f. A statement received monthly from the bank that shows the depositor's bank transactions and balance.

g. A disbursement system that uses wire, telephone, telegraph, or computer to transfer cash from one location to another.

h. Deposits recorded by the depositor that have not been recorded by the bank.

i. Cheques issued and recorded by the company that have not been paid by the bank.

Exercises

E7-1   (SO 4) Avison Company uses a petty cash fund for small cash disbursements. The following transactions occurred during July 2008:

July   1   Established a petty cash fund of $200.

4   Paid freight costs on $52 of goods purchased. The company uses the perpetual inventory system. Issued receipt no.1.

8   Paid $37 in postage expense. Issued receipt no.2.

15   Paid miscellaneous expenses of $29. Issued receipt nos.3 and 4.

20   Paid $44 delivery costs on goods sold. Issued receipt no.5.

24   Paid $35 for office supplies expense. Issued receipt no.6.

25   Replenished petty cash fund by issuing a cheque for $197.

31   Increased petty cash fund to $300.

Instructions

Journalize the entries that affect the Petty Cash account in general journal form.

General Journal			JI
Date	**Account Titles and Explanation**	**Debit**	**Credit**
2008			

E7-2   (SO 4) Merry Cherry Party Company uses a petty cash fund for small cash disbursements. The following transactions occurred during December 2008:

Dec.   1   Established a petty cash fund of $100.

4   Paid $25 for delivery of chairs and tables rented. Issued receipt no.1.

8   Paid $45 in postage expense. Issued receipt no.2.

15   Paid for $20 of special office supplies. Issued receipt no.3.

16   Replenished and increased the petty cash fund by $200 (there was $5 cash left in the petty cash box).

Instructions
Journalize the entries that affect the Petty Cash account in general journal form. Use a compound entry to replenish and increase on December 16.

General Journal			JI
Date	**Account Titles and Explanation**	**Debit**	**Credit**
2008			

E7-3   (SO 6) The following table represents reconciliation items that may occur when doing a bank reconciliation:

	Reconciliation Items	Who knows about this transaction BOOK/BANK?	Add to BOOK	Deduct from BOOK	Add to BANK	Deduct from BANK
1.	Outstanding cheques					
2.	Service charges					
3.	Interest earned and credited to bank account					
4.	Company cheque correctly written for $564 but recorded as $546					
5.	Deposits in transit					
6.	Bank charges to company account in error					
7.	Interest charged to bank account					
8.	Fees charges by bank for NSF cheque					
9.	Bank credit memorandum to company account in error					
10.	Bank debit memorandum to company account					

Instructions

Indicate using the words BANK or BOOK in the first blank column and by a check mark in the remaining columns as to how the items should be treated when doing the bank reconciliation.

E7-4   (SO 6) On April 30, 2009, the Berkeley Company showed a balance of $28,910 in its Cash account. On May 9, Berkeley received its bank statement for the month ended April 30, which showed an ending balance of $32,520. The following items were included on the bank statement:

1. Charges to Berkeley included $115 for the use of a bank safety deposit box and $20 in service charges.
2. Deposits in transit, $4,520.
3. Outstanding cheques: no. 544, $3,220; no. 567, $1,680; and no. 599, $3,000.
4. An NSF cheque from Garvin Saldenas for $3,000 that was received on account was returned with an additional service charge of $25.
5. The bank statement shows an electronic transfer from a customer. Velasquez Company paid $3,390 on account, $390 of which was interest charges.

Instructions
(a) Prepare a bank reconciliation for the Berkeley Company for the month ended April 30, 2009.

_____

_____

BERKELEY COMPANY
Bank Reconciliation
April 30, 2009

(b) Journalize the adjusting entries for Berkeley Company on April 30, 2009.

General Journal			JI
Date	**Account Titles and Explanation**	**Debit**	**Credit**
2008			

E7-5   (SO 6) The following is the general ledger Cash account and the bank statement for the Beethoven Company for the month of January 2009.

BEETHOVEN COMPANY
General Ledger
Cash

Date		Explanation	Ref	Debit	Credit	Balance
2009						
Jan.	1	Balance				$35,030
	1			2,000		
	4	Cheque # 298			150	
		Cheque # 299			2,000	34,880
	5	Cheque # 300			1,450	
		Cheque # 301			3,461	29,969
	16			20,000		
	17			14,500		64,469
	19	Cheque # 302			2,000	62,469
	21	Cheque # 303			500	
		Cheque # 304			750	
		Cheque # 305			1,000	60,219
		Cheque # 306			2,465	
		Cheque # 307			1,789	
		Cheque # 308			2,500	
	25	Cheque # 309			500	52,965
		Cheque # 310			3,000	
	31			4,000		53,965

BEETHOVEN COMPANY
Bank Statement
Janaury 31, 2009

			Cheques and Other Debits	Deposits and Other Credits	Balance
Jan.	1	Balance			39,185
	1			2,000	41,185
	4	Cheque # 297	4,155		37,030
	9	Cheque # 298	150		
		Cheque # 299	2,000		
		Cheque # 300	1,450		
		Cheque # 301	3,416		30,014
	16			20,000	
	17			14,500	64,514
	25	Cheque # 302	2,000		
		Cheque # 303	500		
		Cheque # 304	750		
		Cheque # 306	2,465		
		Cheque # 307	1,789		
	30	Cheque # 309	500		56,510
		EFT customer		1,500	58,010
		NSF cheque	2,990		
		Service charge on NSF	10		
		Other service charge	10		55,000

Additional information:
1. Error: Cheque no. 301 for $3,416 was correctly paid by the bank, but was recorded by the company for $3,461. This cheque was a payment on account to a creditor.
2. The EFT customer is a payment from Chopin Company on account.
3. The NSF cheque is a cheque from a customer, Franz Schubert.

Instructions
(a) Prepare a bank reconciliation for the Beethoven Company at January 31, 2009.

BEETHOVEN COMPANY
Bank Reconciliation
January 31, 2009

(b) Journalize the adjusting entries for Beethoven Company on January 31, 2009.

General Journal			J1
Date	**Account Titles and Explanation**	**Debit**	**Credit**
2008			

Solutions to Review Questions and Exercises

Multiple Choice

1. (d) All three are correct. Internal control is the process that management designs and implements to help an organization achieve reliable financial reporting, effective and efficient operations, and compliance with relevant laws and regulations

2. (c) Answers (a), (b), and (d) are all considered part of good internal control. The responsibility for related transactions should be assigned to different individuals.

3. (d) Independent internal reviews of performance or records involve the review, comparison, and reconciliation of information from two different sources. Answers (a), (b), and (c) are all considered independent internal reviews. Answer (d) has nothing to do with internal reviews and is actually considered poor internal control.

4. (a) Internal auditors are employees of the company who evaluate the effectiveness of the company's system of internal control on a year-round basis. In addition, they review the activities of departments for compliance with prescribed internal controls.

5. (b) Physical controls relate primarily to the safeguarding of assets and include the measures identified in (a), (c), and (d). The bonding of employees who handle cash is a control, but not a physical control.

6. (d) Answers (a), (b), and (c) are effective internal control measures. Permitting collusion among employees gets around prescribed controls and will significantly impair the effectiveness of a system.

7. (b) The human factor (choice (a)) is important because internal control may become ineffective through employee fatigue and indifference. Answer (c) may significantly impair the internal control system because collusion circumvents prescribed controls. No internal control system is infallible (choice (d)).

8. (d) Answers (a), (b), and (c) are valid statements. Answer (d) is a violation of segregation of duties.

9. (a) A cashier department supervisor should make the daily cash count, not the cashiers since they would be checking their own work. Answers (b), (c), and (d) are applications of independent reviews of performance or records.

10. (c) Storing cash in a company safe is an application of physical control.

11. (b) The only true statement is that the retailer is charged a transaction fee for each debit card transaction. Items (a), (c), and (d) are false.

12. (d) Electronic funds transfers limit errors of agreement that can occur with paper documentation and is an effective control factor. Choices (a), (b), and (c) are all effective controls.

13. (b) This choice violates the internal control activity of independent performance reviews. An independent individual should prepare the bank reconciliation.

14. (a) Upon payment, the approved invoice (or form) should be stamped PAID to prevent it from being resubmitted for payment at a later date. Answers (b), (c), and (d) are incorrect. Blank cheques should be stored in a safe, comparison should be made before the cheque is issued, and a cheque signer who also records the cheques is a violation of segregation of duties.

15. (b) Electronic payment of accounts payable can be done by companies and should be checked against a list of authorized electronic payments.

16. (d) No entry is made when a petty cash payment occurs. Each payment, though, must be documented on a pre-numbered petty cash receipt.

17. (b) A debit of $1 to Cash Over and Short is the correct answer. The entry is:

Expenses	92.00	
Cash Over and Short	1.00	
Cash		93.00

18. (d) No accounting entry is necessary; the expense is recognized when the fund is replenished.

19. (c) When the fund is replenished, the amount of the cheque made to replenish the fund is the difference between the original amount of the fund and the amount left in cash. Any difference between the cheque and the receipts in the petty cash fund is either debited or credited to the account Cash Short and Over.

20. (b) Many companies have more than one bank account. They use regional bank accounts, payroll bank accounts, and other accounts to obtain short-term loans.

21. (a) The three parties to a cheque are (1) the maker (or drawer) who issues the cheque, (2) the bank (or payer) on which the cheque is drawn, and (3) the payee to whom the cheque is payable.

22. (a) Deposits should only be made by an authorized employee like the head cashier. This is an essential control activity, ensuring a specific employee is responsible for a specific task.

23. (c) An EFT made to the depositor's account will be recorded as a credit entry on the bank statement. The bank service charge (choice (a)), NSF cheques (choice (b)), and the cost of printing cheques (choice (d)) will all result in a debit entry on the bank statement.

24. (c) Deposits in transit are added to the balance per bank statement, outstanding cheques are deducted from the balance per bank, and NSF cheques are deducted from the balance per books.

25. (a) The bank's records and the depositor's records lack agreement because of time lags and errors that can be made by either party.

26. (b) Cash consists of coins, currency (paper or virtual money), cheques, money orders, and money on deposit in a bank or similar depository. In general, if a bank will accept it for deposit, it is cash. Postdated cheques are classified as accounts receivable.

27. (b) A cash equivalent is defined as a highly liquid investment that can be converted into a specific amount of cash with a maturity of three months or less when purchased.

28. (d) Answers (a), (b), and (c) are all correct. Item (d) is incorrect because cash on hand, cash in banks, and petty cash are normally combined and reported simply as Cash on the balance sheet.

Matching

1.	e.	4.	b.	7.	f.
2.	a.	5.	i.	8.	c.
3.	d.	6.	h.	9.	g.

Exercises

E7-1

General Journal				JI
Date	**Account Titles and Explanation**	**Debit**	**Credit**	
2008				
July 1	Petty Cash	200		
	Cash		200	
	To establish the petty cash fund.			
25	Merchandise Inventory	52		
	Postage Expense	37		
	Miscellaneous Expense	29		
	Delivery Expense	44		
	Office Supplies Expense	35		
	Cash		197	
	To replenish the petty cash fund.			
31	Petty Cash	100		
	Cash		100	
	To increase the petty cash fund.			

E7-2

General Journal			JI
Date	**Account Titles and Explanation**	**Debit**	**Credit**
2008			
Dec 1	Petty Cash	100	
	Cash		100
	To establish the petty cash fund.		
16	Delivery Expense	25	
	Postage Expense	45	
	Office Supplies Expense	20	
	Cash Over and Short	5	
	Petty Cash	200	
	Cash		295
	To replenish and increase petty cash fund.		

E7-3

	Reconciliation Items	Who knows about this transaction BOOK/BANK?	Add to BOOK	Deduct from BOOK	Add to BANK	Deduct from BANK
1.	Outstanding cheques	BOOK				✓
2.	Service charges	BANK		✓		
3.	Interest earned and credited to bank account	BANK	✓			
4.	Company cheque correctly written for $564 but recorded as $546	BOOK		✓		
5.	Deposits in transit	BOOK			✓	
6.	Bank charges to company account in error	BANK			✓	
7.	Interest charged to bank account	BANK		✓		
8.	Fees charges by bank for NSF cheque	BANK		✓		
9.	Bank credit memorandum to company account in error	BANK				✓
10.	Bank debit memorandum to company account	BANK	✓			

E7-4

(a)

BERKELEY COMPANY
Bank Reconciliation
April 30, 2009

Cash balance per bank statement			$32,520
Add:	Deposits in transit		4,520
			37,040
Less:	Outstanding cheques:		
	No. 544	$3,220	
	No. 567	1,680	
	No. 399	3,000	7,900
Adjusted cash balance per bank			$29,140
Cash balance per books			$28,910
Add:	Electronic transfer per bank statement		3,390
			32,300
Less:	NSF cheque	$3,025	
	Bank service charge	135	3,160
Adjusted cash balance per books			$29,140

(b)

General Journal			JI
Date	**Account Titles and Explanation**	**Debit**	**Credit**
2009			
Apr. 30	Cash	3,390	
	Accounts Receivable—Velasquez		3,000
	Interest Revenue		390
	To record transfer of funds per statement.		
30	Accounts Receivable—Saldenas	3,025	
	Cash		3,025
	To record return of NSF cheque and service charges.		
30	Bank Service Charge Expense	135	
	Cash		135
	To record service charges.		

E7-5
(a)

BEETHOVEN COMPANY
Bank Reconciliation
January 31, 2009

Cash balance per bank statement			$55,000
Add:	Deposits in transit		4,000
			59,000
Less:	Outstanding cheques		
	No. 305	$1,000	
	No. 308	2,500	
	No. 310	3,000	6,500
Adjusted cash balance per bank			$52,500
Cash balance per books			$53,965
Add:	Electronic transfer per bank statement	$1,500	
	Error in recording cheque no.301 ($3,461 – $3,416)	45	1,545
			55,510
Less:	NSF cheque ($2,990 + $10)	$3,000	
	Bank service charge	10	3,010
Adjusted cash balance per books			$52,500

(b)

General Journal			JI
Date	**Account Titles and Explanation**	**Debit**	**Credit**
2009			
Jan. 31	Cash	1,500	
	Accounts Receivable—Chopin		1,500
	To record the transfer of funds from		
	customer.		
31	Cash	45	
	Accounts Payable		45
	To correct error in recording cheque		
	No. 301.		
31	Accounts Receivable—Franz Schubert	3,000	
	Cash		3,000
	To record NSF cheque & service charge.		
31	Bank Charges Expense	10	
	Cash		10
	To record January bank service charge.		